John Alonzo Fisher

An Illustrated Record of the Retrospective Exhibition Held at South Kensington

1896

John Alonzo Fisher

An Illustrated Record of the Retrospective Exhibition Held at South Kensington
1896

ISBN/EAN: 9783744659031

Printed in Europe, USA, Canada, Australia, Japan

Cover: Foto ©ninafisch / pixelio.de

More available books at **www.hansebooks.com**

An Illustrated Record

OF THE

Retrospective Exhibition

HELD AT . . . .

SOUTH KENSINGTON, 1896

COMPILED AND EDITED

BY

∽ JOHN FISHER ∾

HEAD MASTER
KENSINGTON SCHOOL OF
SCIENCE & ART, BERKELEY
SQUARE, BRISTOL ∾ ∾

CONTAINING TWO HUNDRED AND FIFTY-SIX
ILLUSTRATIONS OF DESIGNS, MODELS, PAINT-
INGS, DRAWINGS FROM LIFE, ETC., FOR WHICH
GOLD AND SILVER MEDALS HAVE BEEN AWARDED
BY THE DEPARTMENT OF SCIENCE AND ART

London: CHAPMAN & HALL, Ld.
1897

An Illustrated Record of the Retrospective Exhibition held at South Kensington, 1896.

N venturing to place before the public this illustrated record of the Retrospective Exhibition of 1896, we are actuated by the following objects :—

1. To preserve in permanent form, for the immediate use of art masters, teachers, students, designers, modellers, draughtsmen, and art workmen generally, the principal examples which compose this instructive and interesting exhibition, all of which have within the past eleven years been awarded Gold and Silver Medals by the Department of Science and Art.

2. To effect a direct connection between the art student and the manufacturer, by providing the latter with a handy means of reference, and be to them an indication of the best exponents of the particular kind of art work they demand.

3. To visibly demonstrate and record the growth and progress of our art schools and English practical art in general.

The progress of practical art, particularly at the present time, offers one of the most interesting studies of the day. On all sides we hear discussed the merits and demerits of technical education, how and in what way it is to affect our workmen, our manufacturers, our art schools: even our daily comforts are to be influenced! And as the art school has been, and is, the vitalising stimulus to the technical education movement of to-day, it is opportune that the Retrospective Exhibition at South Kensington which

was organised

was organized by the Department of Science and Art, and opened in July 1896, should, by a work of this nature, be commemorated as of the greatest interest, usefulness, and necessity.

The great interest taken by Her Majesty the Queen, and the late Prince Consort, in the development of Art in this country, renders the publication of this work in the sixtieth year of her reign, and following upon an international commemoration of the longest reign of any English sovereign, one of peculiar significance and interest, and offers another tribute to Her Majesty's wisdom when, in November 1852, in a speech at the opening of Parliament, she stated that "The advancement of the fine "arts and of practical science will be readily recognised by you as worthy "the attention of a great and enlightened nation. I have directed that "a comprehensive scheme shall be laid before you, having in view the "promotion of these objects, towards which I invite your aid and "co-operation." The policy thus indicated took form in the creation of the Department of Science and Art in the following year.

A brief retrospect of the origin of our art schools and classes will probably be of interest, and by its introduction in these notes the growth and progress will be better understood.

In the year 1835, in response to a motion proposed in the House of Commons by Mr. William Ewart, M.P. for Liverpool, a select committee was appointed, and in 1836, on the reappointment of the committee, the establishment of schools of design was recommended.

As a result of this recommendation, the Treasury voted £1500 for the establishment of a normal school of design, which was opened in Somerset House on the 1st of June, 1837.

In 1841 the Government decided to assist in the formation and maintenance of schools of design in the manufacturing centres, and voted an annual grant for this purpose.

In 1851-52 there were seventeen branch schools, and in the latter year the Managing Council was abolished, and in its place was created a Department of Practical Art, which, on the addition of a science division a year later, changed its title to that of the Department of Science and Art.

Constitutional changes continued to be made, the principal one being the amalgamation of the Education and Science and Art Departments in 1856. Previous to this change the Department of Science and Art was under the direction of the Board of Trade. On the amalgamation of the two establishments, they were placed under the Lord President of the Council, a Vice-President, and a Committee of the Council on Education.

In 1857 the Department took up its abode at South Kensington, having removed from Marlborough House, where, on leaving Somerset House in 1852, it had been located. At the time of its removal to South Kensington there were 12,509 students receiving instruction in local schools of Art, and 396 at the National Art Training School, whereas only 6,997 students attended the schools of design previous to the establishment of the Department. The official report shows that in 1895 there were 136,768 receiving instruction in our art schools and classes.

In arranging the Retrospective Exhibition, the Department at once hit upon the best method of showing the value of its organisation and work, and to disprove that oft-repeated fallacy—the supremacy in Art of our Continental neighbours. Work for work, and school for school, it will be difficult indeed to verify the statements which we hear so easily and airily made about the quality of the practical art work of our country as compared with that of France and Germany.

In this publication, as in the Exhibition itself, the value and progress of the art teaching in our schools of art is shown in actuality; devoid of all embellishments, each work is exhibited on its merits.

The effect on the student of the perpetuation of the Exhibition will be most valuable, and for years to come, consciously or otherwise, its influence will assert itself.

On the art master and teacher the suggestive usefulness will be apparent in our national competitions. Birth will be given to new and enlarged ideas, a better understanding with the work done and the work to do, an enlightenment as to the strength and weakness of their individual positions, and an encouraging stimulus in that the labour they are called upon to undertake is surely and rapidly building for this country a national art, which by its purity and simplicity will in years to come demonstrate the supremacy of English practical art.

To the manufacturer, it will be difficult to overestimate the value of this collection of art work. In other exhibitions good and bad are so intermingled that debased examples unfortunately leave an impression which almost, if not entirely, obliterates the simpler æsthetic qualities. which are alone the properties of pure art.

To the designer, on whom the manufacturer has to depend for his original ideas, the influence must be far-reaching and acceptable, and should tend, as it were, to weld together the artist and the manufacturer into one enlightened person, working and striving for the advancement of the beautiful and the practical.

It is, however, in the interest of the students that this lasting memorial of the Retrospective Exhibition has been undertaken. They are, or soon will be, the art workmen on whom so much will depend. If English Art is to be universally acknowledged as a fact, if supremacy is to be obtained and retained, it is the art student, by his thorough knowledge, his enthusiasm, and his desire for the best, and nothing but the best, that will accomplish it.

List of Illustrations.

NOTE.
G. M. . . . Gold Medal. | S. M. . . . Silver Medal.
S. Kensington. . . . South Kensington.

					PLATES
ALBROW, O. R. .	. S. M. 1884 .	Great Yarmouth .	. *Damask*	.	35
ALLEN, H. .	. G. M. 1886 .	Warrington .	. *Carpet* .	.	41
ANDERSON, EMILY	. S. M. 1888 .	Cork .	. *Carrickmacross Lace* .		4
ANDERSON, EMILY	. S. M. 1889 .	Cork .	. *Set Carrickmacross Lace*		5
ANDERSON, EMILY	. S. M. 1889 .	Cork .	. *Set of Lace Designs* .	.	20
ANDERSON, EMILY	. S. M. 1893 .	Cork .	. *Historic Studies of Lace* .	.	104
ANDERSON, EMILY	. S. M. 1891 .	Cork . .	. *Set of Designs for Lace* .		3
ANDERSON, EMILY	. S. M. 1893 .	Cork . .	. *Set of Designs for Lace* .		7
APPLEYARD, F. .	. S. M. 1894 .	Scarborough .	. *Wall-paper* .	. .	58
ASHTON, CLARA B.	. S. M. 1886 .	Manchester, Cav. St.	. *Cotton Hanging* .	.	31
ATHERTON, J. .	. S. M. 1892 .	Bradford .	. *Historic Study* .	.	102
AYLWARD, C. B. .	. G. M. 1884 .	S. Kensington .	. *Set of Carpet Designs* .	.	39
AYLWARD, C. B. .	. G. M. 1884 .	S. Kensington .	. *Set of Carpet Designs* .	.	40
AYLWARD, C. B. .	. G. M. 1884 .	S. Kensington .	. *Set of Carpet Designs* .		50
BAILY, ALICE .	. S. M. 1884 .	Dublin .	. *Flounce* .	.	11
BARRETT, T. .	. S. M. 1884 .	Macclesfield .	. *Silk Hanging* .	.	36
BARRETT, T. .	. S. M. 1889 .	Macclesfield .	*Carpet Design* .	.	51
BARTLETT, M. B. .	S. M. 1890 .	Sheffield .	. *Design for Plaque* .	.	81
BATTERS, EMILY .	. S. M. 1888 .	Hertford .	. *Design for Tiles* .	.	69
BATTERS, EMILY .	. S. M. 1887 .	Hertford .	. *Design for Tiles* .	.	70
BIDDLE, EDITH S.	. S. M. 1891 .	Birmingham .	. *Antique Drawing* .	.	115
BLOCK, HYMAN .	. S. M. 1887 .	Birkbeck Institute .	*Life Drawing* .	.	113
BROTHERS, EMILY C.	. S. M. 1890 .	Canterbury .	. *Silk Hanging* .	.	28
BROWNSWORD, J. J.	. S. M. 1885 .	S. Kensington .	. *Natural History Studies*		92
BRYDEN, R. .	. G. M. 1890 .	S. Kensington .	. *Chalk Drawing (Antique)* .		114
BUTCHER, LAURA .	. S. M. 1888 .	Wakefield .	. *Studies of Drapery* .	.	123
CALDWELL, MARY	G. M. 1893 .	Canterbury .	. *Mosaic Pavement* .		66
CARDER, G. J.	. S. M. 1894 .	Wordsley .	. *Mosaic Pavement* .		71

CARDER, A. H.

viii

				PLATES
CARDER, A. H.	S. M. 1894	Wordsley	Porcelain Vase	130
CARDER, F.	S. M. 1890	Wordsley	Bust of Boy	127
CARDER, G. J.	S. M. 1895	Wordsley	Frame (Modelled)	139
CARPENTER, A. A.	S. M. 1894	Birkbeck Institute	Wall-paper, etc.	54
CARPENTER, A. A.	S. M. 1895	Birkbeck Institute	Wall-paper, etc.	55
CARTLIDGE, G.	S. M. 1891	S. Kensington	Studies of Relief Ornament	94
CARTLIDGE, G.	S. M. 1891	S. Kensington	Studies of Relief Ornament	95
CASSIDY, J.	S. M. 1885	Manchester, Cav. St.	Mod. Panel of Commerce	151
CLARK, W.	S. M. 1886	Macclesfield	Silk Hanging	31
CLOUGH, F. M.	S. M. 1894	Bradford Church Inst.	Ornament in Monochrome	90
COLE, HERBERT	G. M. 1888	Manchester	Set of Carpet Designs	45
COLE, HERBERT	G. M. 1888	Manchester	Set of Carpet Designs	49
COLLINGWOOD, J. H.	S. M. 1895	Battersea	Carpet Design	44
COLLINGWOOD, J. H.	S. M. 1893	Battersea	Monochrome Painting	61
CROMPTON, EDWARD	S. M. 1885	S. Kensington	Plaster Frieze	144
CURTIS, MARY K.	S. M. 1891	Canterbury	Mosaic Pavement	63
CURTIS, MARY K.	S. M. 1889	Canterbury	Mosaic Pavement	63
DABIS, ANNA	S. M. 1886	S. Kensington	Portion of Pediment	151
DALTON, WM. B.	S. M. 1894	S. Kensington	Stoneware Filter	130
DAVIS, CLARA B.	S. M. 1893	Birmingham	Lace Fans	2
DIXON, A. W. L.	S. M. 1886	Nottingham	Carpet Design	38
DONOHUE, T. J.	G. M. 1887	Macclesfield	Tapestry Design	26
DONOHUE, T. J.	G. M. 1888	Macclesfield	Wall-paper	59
DUFFIELD, J. H.	G. M. 1895	Sheffield	Historic Studies of Gold and Silver Objects	97
DUFFIELD, J. H.	G. M. 1895	Sheffield	Historic Studies of Gold and Silver Objects	98
EDGAR, MRS. T. H., née CAROLINE BEATSON	G. M. 1888	Cork	Curtain in Cut Linen	19
EDGAR, MRS. T. H.	S. M. 1887	Cork	Lace Handkerchief, etc.	12
EDGAR, MRS. T. H.	S. M. 1887	Cork	Panel for Lady's Dress, etc.	13
EVANS, WM. E.	S. M. 1888	Hornsey	Study of Head in Chalk	117
FABIAN, E.	G. M. 1888	S. Kensington	Model from Life	135
FENN, W. A.	S. M. 1895	New Cross	Biscuit Box and Silver Cup	82
FENN, W. A.	S. M. 1893	New Cross	Details of Hall Decorations	77
FENN, W. A.	S. M. 1893	New Cross	Details of Hall Decorations	85
FISHER, LAURA M.	G. M. 1892	Clapham	Life Drawing	107
FISHER, A.	S. M. 1886	S. Kensington	Plate with Figure of Cupid	80

				PLATES
S. M. 1886	Glasgow	Carpets (set)	.	47
S. M. 1891	Hertford	Mosaic Pavement	.	71
S. M. 1891	Hertford	Tiles	.	68
S. M. 1893	Hertford	Mosaic Pavements	.	67
S. M. 1893	Hertford	Tiles	.	70
S. M. 1892	Birmingham	Modelled Fish Panel	.	136
G. M. 1891	S. Kensington	Stained Glass Window	.	73
S. M. 1893	Edinburgh	Model from Life	.	156
S. M. 1884	Birmingham	Life Drawings	.	106
S. M. 1884	Birmingham	Life Drawings	.	111
S. M. 1893	S. Kensington	Set of Natural History Studies		91
S. M. 1893	S. Kensington	Set of Natural History Studies		92
G. M. 1892	S. Kensington	Model from Life	.	138
G. M. 1893	S. Kensington	Decorative Model Figure	.	129
G. M. 1892	S. Kensington	Modelled Frieze	.	150
S. M. 1889	Glasgow	Wall-paper	.	53
S. M. 1887	Manchester, Cav. St.	Hanging	.	29
S. M. 1887	Manchester, Cav. St.	Hanging	.	40
S. M. 1884	Macclesfield	Silk Hanging	.	35
S. M. 1890	Glasgow	Plaster Panels	.	126
S. M. 1889	Leicester, Hastings St.	Studies of Drapery	.	121
S. M. 1894	Leicester	Studies of Drapery	.	120
G. M. 1893	Clapham	Life Drawing	.	109
G. M. 1892	Clapham	Life Drawing	.	110
G. M. 1892	Clapham	Life Drawings	.	112
G. M. 1893	S. Kensington	Dado of Curtain	.	57
S. M. 1891	Sheffield	Silver Design	.	86
S. M. 1894	S. Kensington	Antique Drawing	.	115
S. M. 1884	Macclesfield	Silk Hanging	.	30
G. M. 1890	Burnley	Printed Cotton Design	.	24
S. M. 1889	Burnley	Printed Cotton Design	.	25
S. M. 1891	Dublin	Plaster Panel	.	147
G. M. 1890	Dublin	Modelled Frieze	.	137
S. M. 1895	Holloway	Studies of Drapery	.	118
S. M. 1895	Holloway	Drapery Study	.	119
S. M. 1895	Dublin	Set of Lace Designs	.	16

JACOB, ALICE.

					PLATES
Jacob, Alice	.	S. M. 1895 .	Dublin	. Design for Lace .	. 17
Jacob, Alice	.	S. M. 1895 .	Dublin	. Sets of Lace Designs	. 21
Jacob, Alice	.	S. M. 1895 .	Dublin	. Set of Lace Designs	. 15
Jacob, Alice	.	S. M.	Dublin	. Cut Linen Curtain	. 6
Jahn, Albert	.	G. M. 1884 .	Hanley .	. Life Drawing .	. 108
Jewsbury, Margaret	.	S. M. 1895 .	Southport .	. Historic Studies of Lace .	. 103
Johnson, Laura .	.	G. M. 1895 .	Nottingham .	. Painting in Monochrome	. 116
Jones, M. E.	.	G. M. 1886 .	Manchester .	. Stair Carpet Design	. 48
Keppie, Jessie	.	S. M. 1889 .	Glasgow .	. Carpet Design	. 51
Kerr, T. .	.	S. M. 1884 .	Macclesfield	Silk Hanging	30
King, J. J. F.	.	G. M. 1888 .	Glasgow .	. Carpet Design	. 37
King, J. J. F.	.	G. M. 1888 .	Glasgow .	. Carpet Detail	. 38
Knight, W. H. .	.	S. M. 1895 .	Birmingham .	. Life Drawing .	. 113
Kwialkowski, A. J.	.	S. M. 1890 .	Hanley .	. Porcelain Vase	. 152
Lake, Gertrude .	.	G. M. 1891 .	Manchester, Cav. St. .	. Interior in Oils .	. 88
Latimer, J. .	.	S. M. 1886 .	Manchester, Cav. St. .	. Printed Cotton Hanging	. 45
Light, Kate	.	S. M. 1893 .	S. Kensington .	. Figure Panels .	. 76
Lomax, Helen .	.	S. M. 1896 .	Manchester, Cav. St. .	. Cotton Hangings .	. 27
Macfarlane, J. .	.	S. M. 1886 .	Manchester, Cav. St. .	. Gates, Iron .	. 83
Marley, Agnes .	.	S. M. 1895 .	Birmingham .	. Window Filling .	. 74
Mason, J. .	.	S. M. 1892 .	Birmingham .	. Plaster Panel .	. 146
Mawson, S. G.	.	S. M. 1885 .	Manchester, Cav. St.	. Printed Cotton Hanging	. 33
Mawson, S. G.	.	G. M. 1884 .	Manchester, Cav. St. .	. Printed Cotton Hangings	. 34
Mawson, S. G.	.	G. M. 1884 .	Manchester, Cav. St. .	. Printed Cotton Hanging	. 36
Mawson, S. G.	.	G. M. 1886 .	Manchester, Cav. St. .	. Wall-paper .	. 52
McCrossan, Peter	.	G. M.	S. Kensington .	. Plaster Panel .	. 128
M'Gill, David	.	S. M. 1891 .	S. Kensington .	. Medal Designs (Modelled)	. 155
M'Gill, David	.	G. M. 1890 .	S. Kensington .	. Figure Composition .	. 153
M'Kechnie, C. W.	.	S. M. 1889 .	Birmingham.	. Spandril, Terra Cotta .	. 149
Mercer, Eleanor L.	.	G. M. 1894 .	Sheffield .	. Historic Studies .	. 96
Mercer, Eleanor L. .	.	G. M. 1894 .	Sheffield .	. Gold and Silver Goblet .	. 124
Mills, A. .	.	S. M. 1895 .	S. Kensington .	. Model in Relief from Life	. 134
Mohun, Mary .	.	S. M. 1890 .	Canterbury .	. Tiles (set) .	. 72
Möller, Oscar P.	.	S. M. 1895 .	Battersea .	. Frieze .	. 61
Moore, F. G. .	.	S. M. 1885 .	Manchester, Cav. St. .	. Wrought-iron Gates .	. 83
Moore, Esther .	.	S. M. 1893 .	S. Kensington .	. Decorative Figure (Modelled)	141

				PLATES
S. M. 1891	. Hanley .	. Porcelain Vase .	.	. 152
S. M. 1893	. S. Kensington	. Damask Table-cloth	.	. 23
S. M. 1886	. Birmingham	. Head from Life, in Chalk		. 117
S. M. 1893	. Glasgow .	. Wall-paper .		55
S. M. 1895	. Birmingham	. Stained Glass		. 75
S. M. 1892	. Bradford	. Lace Fans .		2
S. M.	. Glasgow	. Historic Studies of Tapestry		. 105
G. M. 1886	. Lambeth .	. Terra Cotta Panel		. 132
S. M. 1895	. Birmingham	Study of Drapery .		. 122
S. M. 1889	. Birmingham	. Design for Figure Panels		. 78
S. M. 1894	. Wordsley .	. Ceiling. . .		. 139
S. M. 1889	. Nottingham .	. Lace Design .		1
S. M. 1889	. Nottingham .	. Lace Design . .		. 22
S. M. 1892	. Nottingham .	. Lace Designs .		8
S. M. 1892	. S. Kensington	. Designs for Wrought Iron		. 84
S. M. 1895	. Cork . .	. Lace Design . .		. 9
S. M. 1895	. Cork . .	. Lace Design . .		17
S. M. 1885	. Manchester .	. Design for Hanging		. 32
S. M. 1886	. Manchester .	. Design for Cotton Hanging		. 29
S. M. 1891	. Burnley .	. Design for Cotton Hanging		. 33
S. M. 1887	. S. Kensington	. Design for Caryatide .		. 145
S. M. 1884	. Lambeth .	. Design for Plaster Panel		. 149
G. M. 1891	. Canterbury .	. Mosaic Pavement .		. 62
G. M. 1891	. Canterbury .	. Mosaic Pavement .		64
G. M. 1892	. Canterbury .	. Mosaic Pavement .		. 65
G. M. 1891	. Canterbury .	. Design for Tiles .		. 68
G. M. 1890	. Canterbury . .	. Design for Plaque		. 81
S. M. 1888	. Manchester, Cav. St.	. Printed Hanging .		. 28
S. M. 1893	. Glasgow	Wall-paper . .		53
S. M. 1890	. Derby .	. Study of Pottery .		. 100
S. M. 1890	. Derby . .	. Study of Pottery . .		. 101
S. M. 1885	. Manchester .	. Design for Hanging .		. 32
G. M. 1895	. Kensington Sch., Bristol	Panel based on a Celery Plant		140
S. M. 1885	. S. Kensington .	. Design for Plateau .		. 79
S. M. 1887	. Manchester .	. Frieze in Plaster .		. 144

SHUKER, F.

					PLATES
SHUKER, F.	S. M. 1894	Wordsley	Plaster Frieze		147
SIMPSON, M. L.	G. M.	S. Kensington	Book Cover in Pierced Silver		143
SIMPSON, M. L.	G. M. 1895	S. Kensington	Bronze Candlestick		125
SIMPSON, M. L.	S. M. 1893	S. Kensington	Decorative Figure, Modelled		141
SKEAPING, KENNETH	S. M. 1884	Liverpool	Chalk Drawing from Life		111
STEELE, FLORENCE	S. M. 1895	S. Kensington	Design for Tiles		133
STEELE, FLORENCE	G. M. 1896	S. Kensington	Design for Book Cover in Silver		148
STEELE, FLORENCE	S. M. 1895	S. Kensington	Design for a Silver Goblet		127
STEELEY, F.	S. M. 1891	Birmingham	Design for a Jewel Casket		86
STEEN, ANNIE	S. M. 1891	Birmingham	Design for Lace		18
STRANG, MAGGIE	G. M. 1889	Glasgow	Wall-paper		56
SUDDARDS, F.	G. M. 1889	S. Kensington	Portrait in Oil		87
SWAN, F. A. E.	S. M. 1891	Manchester	Studies of Drapery		121
THORNHILL, CAROLINE	S. M. 1894	Blackheath	Wall-papers		60
TRATMAN, TRACY	S. M. 1885	S. Kensington	Studies of Pottery Border		89
TWISS, J. M.	S. M. 1896	S. Kensington	Ornament in Monochrome		90
TWISS, J. M.	S. M.	S. Kensington	Designs based on a Daisy		133
TWISS, J. M.	S. M. 1895	S. Kensington	Model of Relief from Life		134
URWIN, W. C.	G. M. 1892	S. Kensington	Model from Life, in Relief		154
VINALL, J. W. T.	S. M. 1894	S. Kensington	Studies of Fish, etc.		93
WALKER, A.	S. M. 1895	Glasgow	Window Design		74
WALKER, A.	S. M. 1895	Glasgow	Window Design		75
WALKER, A.	S. M. 1895	Glasgow	Window Design		76
WALKER, A.	G. M. 1890	Glasgow	Carpet Design		46
WALKER, A.	G. M. 1890	Glasgow	Carpet Designs		42
WALKER, A.	G. M. 1890	Glasgow	Carpet Designs (set)		43
WATSON, A.	G. M. 1894	Birmingham	Model from Life		131
WHEATLEY, O.	S. M. 1893	Birmingham	Designs for Medals		155
WHITESIDE, ROSA C.	S. M. 1891	Bloomsbury	Study in Water Colours		89
WILLIS, S. A.	S. M. 1894	Plymouth	Wall Tiles, Modelled		136
WILLOUGHBY, E.	G. M. 1895	Plymouth	Modelled Wall Decorations		142
WINSER, M.	S. M. 1893	Dover	Design for Lace (set)		10
WINSER, M.	S. M. 1894	Dover	Design for Lace		9
WINSER, M.	S. M. 1894	Dover	Design for Lace		14
WINSER, M.	S. M. 1893	Dover	Design for Lace (set)		18
WOOD, MILLY	S. M.	Leeds	Study of Drapery in Chalk		123

DESIGNS FOR LACE.

Plates 1 to 22.

Design for Lace Handkerchief.

Design for Lace.

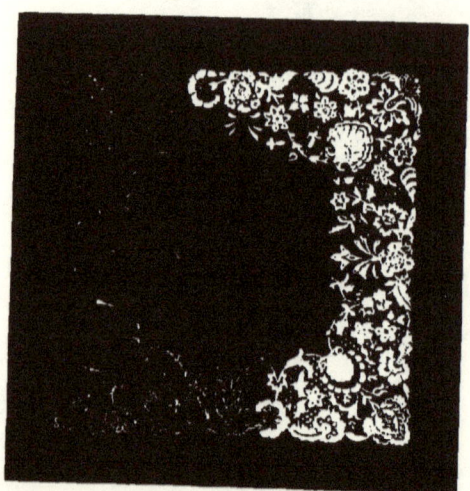

Design for Curtain. Cut Linen and Embroidery.

ALICE JACOB, DUBLIN

7

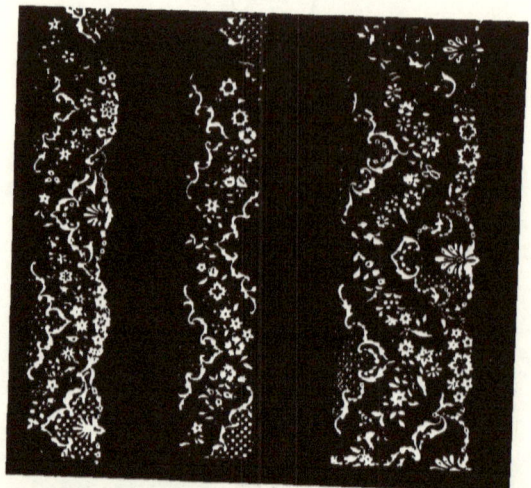

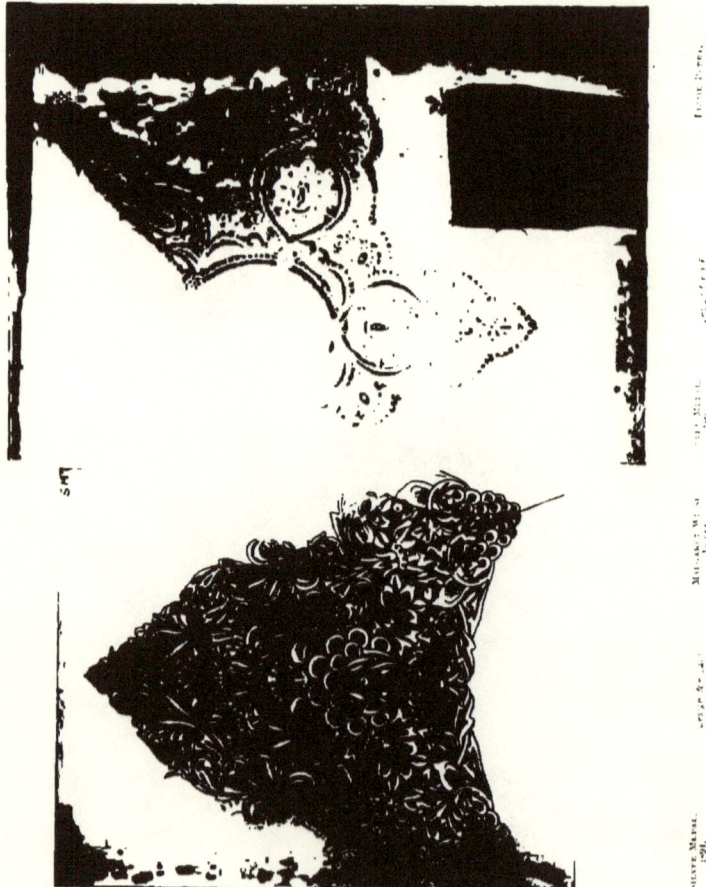

10

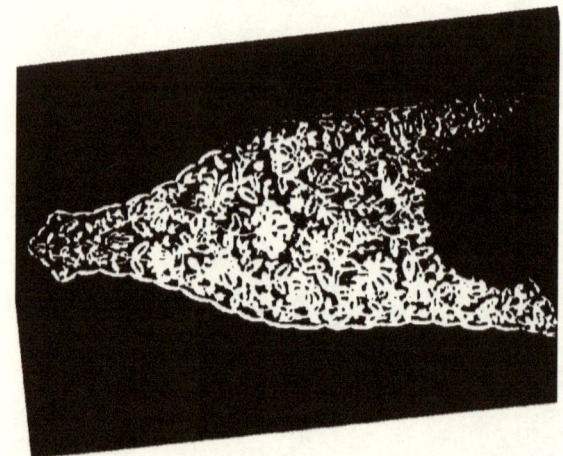

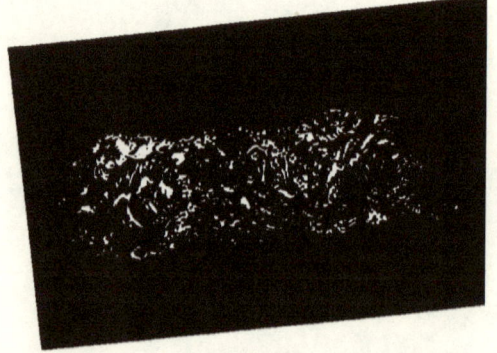

11

Design for Flounce.

SILVER MEDAL. Design for Handkerchief. ALICE BAILY,
1881.   DUBLIN.

12

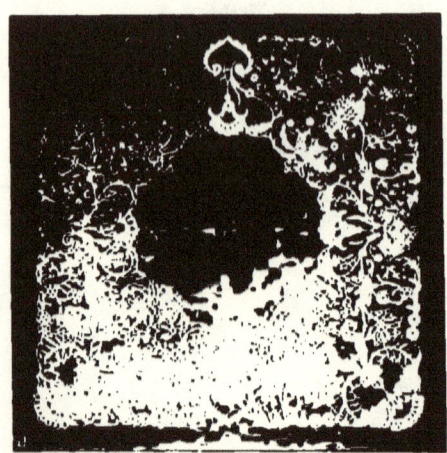

Design for Panel for Lady's Dress.

SILVER MEDAL, 1897.   Design for a Frieze.   MRS. J. H. EDGAR, NEWRY, née CAROLINE C. BEATTY, COLE.

14

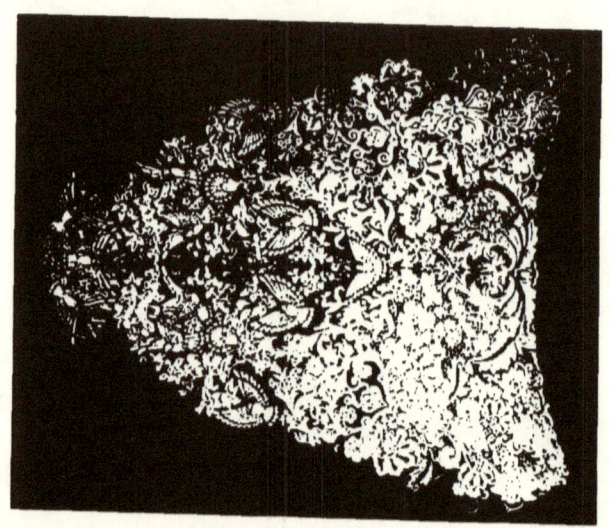

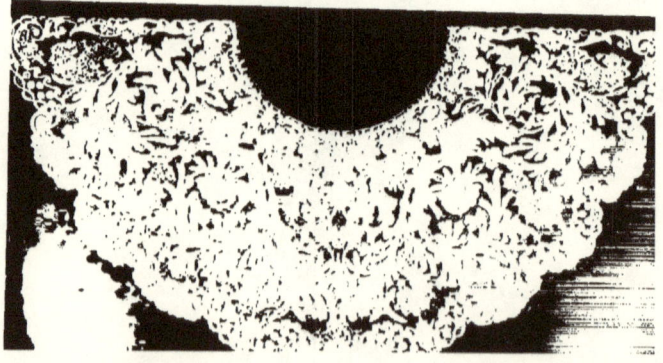

15

SILVER MEDAL, 1897.   Designs for Flounces in Carrickmacross Guipure   ALICE JACOB, DUBLIN.

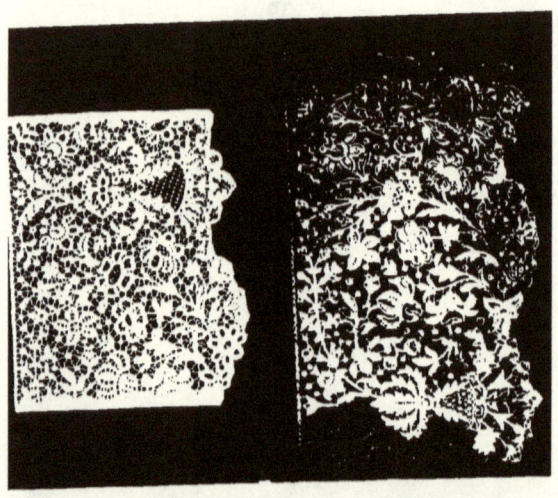

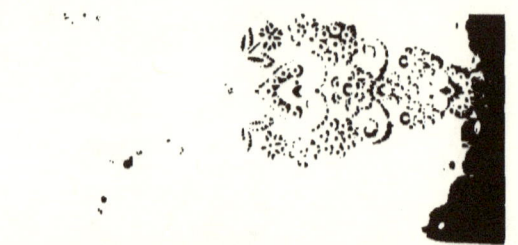

Design for Fichu in Crochet Lace — LIZZIE PERRY, CORK.

18

Design for Curtain in Cut Linen.

SILVER MEDAL,
1880.

EMILY ANDERSON,
CORK.

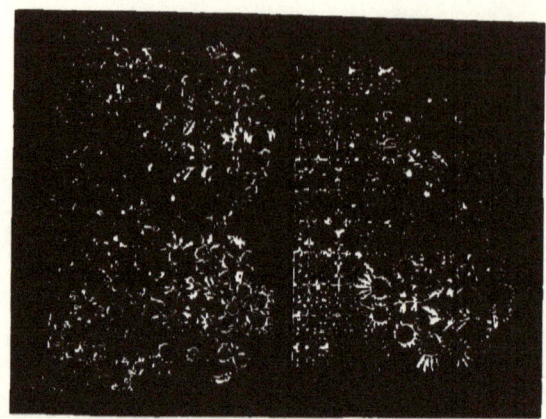

Crochet Design

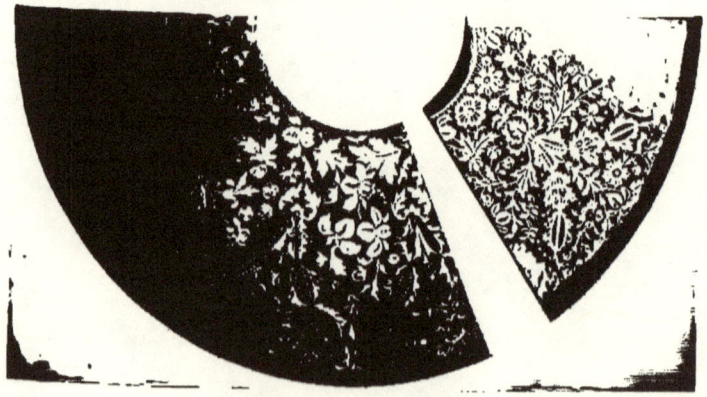

SILVER MEDAL.
1-93

Design for Lace Fan.

ALICE JACOB,
DUBLIN.

ER MEDAL,   Design for Cut Linen Lace.   W. H. PEGG,
NOTTINGHAM

DESIGNS FOR FABRICS.

Plates 23 to 36.

23

SILVER MEDAL, 1893.   Designs for Damask Table Covers.   S. H. MOSS, SOUTH KENSINGTON.

Gold Medal, 1890. *Design for Printed Cotton Hanging*. W. E. Holt, Burnley.

25

SILVER MEDAL.   Design for Printed Cotton Hanging.   R. HOLT,
BURNLEY.

Design for Tapestry.

27

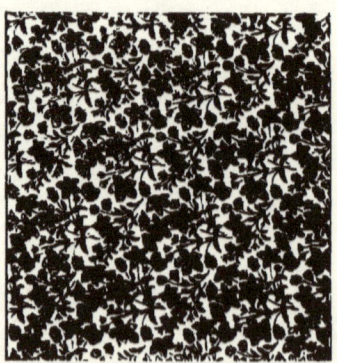

Silver Medal, 1896.   *Designs for Cotton Hangings.*   Helen Lowan, Manchester.

28

SILVER MEDAL, 1890.   Design for Silk Hanging.   EMILY C. BROTHERS, CANTERBURY.

SILVER MEDAL, 1888.   Design for Printed Hanging.   FANNY A. BOYLANCE, MANCHESTER (Cavendish St.)

Silver Medal,
1886.

C. Procopides,
Manchester (Cavendish St.)

Silver Medal,
1887.

Cotton Hanging.

Jane B. Glanvill,
Manchester (Cavendish St.)

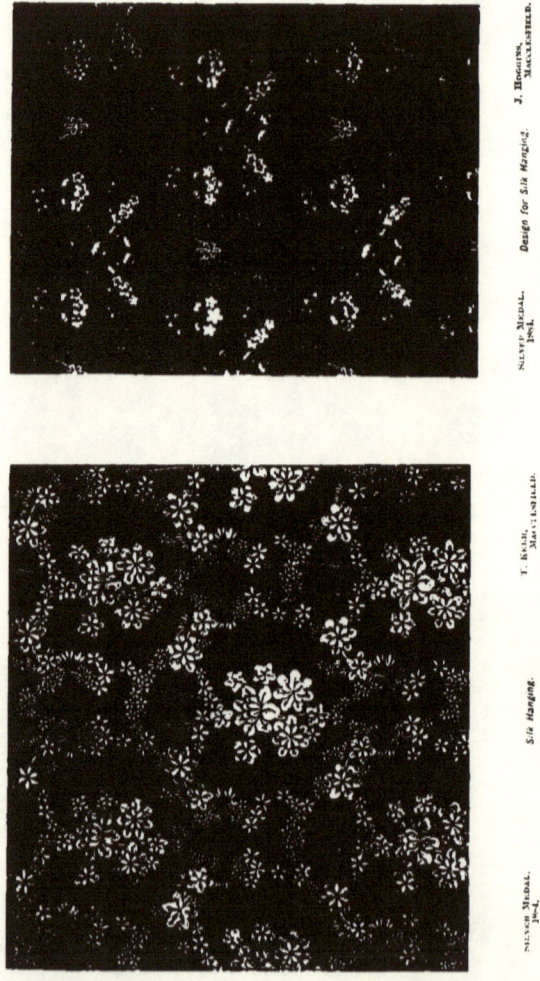

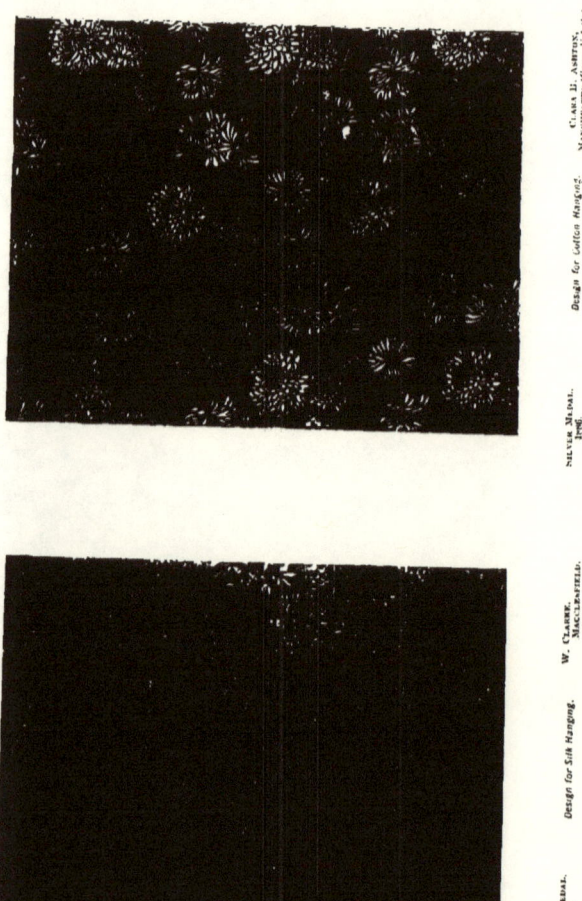

SWANSEA SCHOFIELD, MANCHESTER (Cavendish St.) *Design for Hanging.* SILVER MEDAL, 1885.

C. PROCTOR & Co., MANCHESTER (Cavendish St.) *Design for Hanging.* SILVER MEDAL, 1885.

33

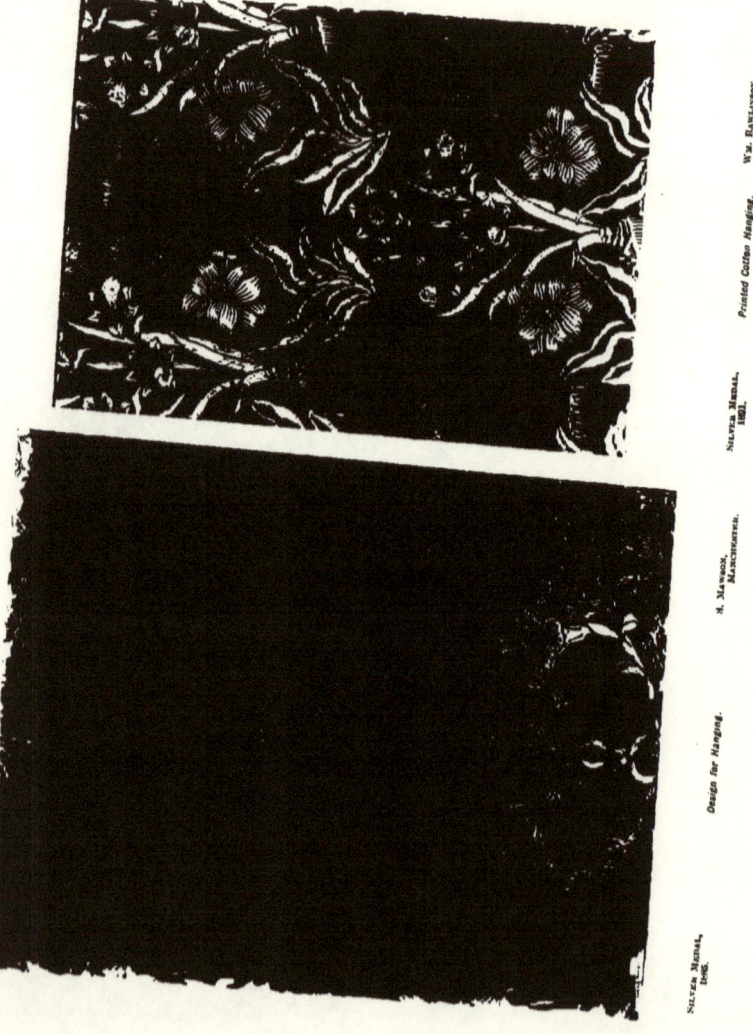

Silver Medal, 1845. Design for Hanging. S. Mawson, Manchester. Silver Medal, 1851. Printed Cotton Hanging. Wm. Rawlinson, Burnley.

Gold Medal, 1901.   *Printed Hanging*   Sidney G. Mawson, Manchester

35

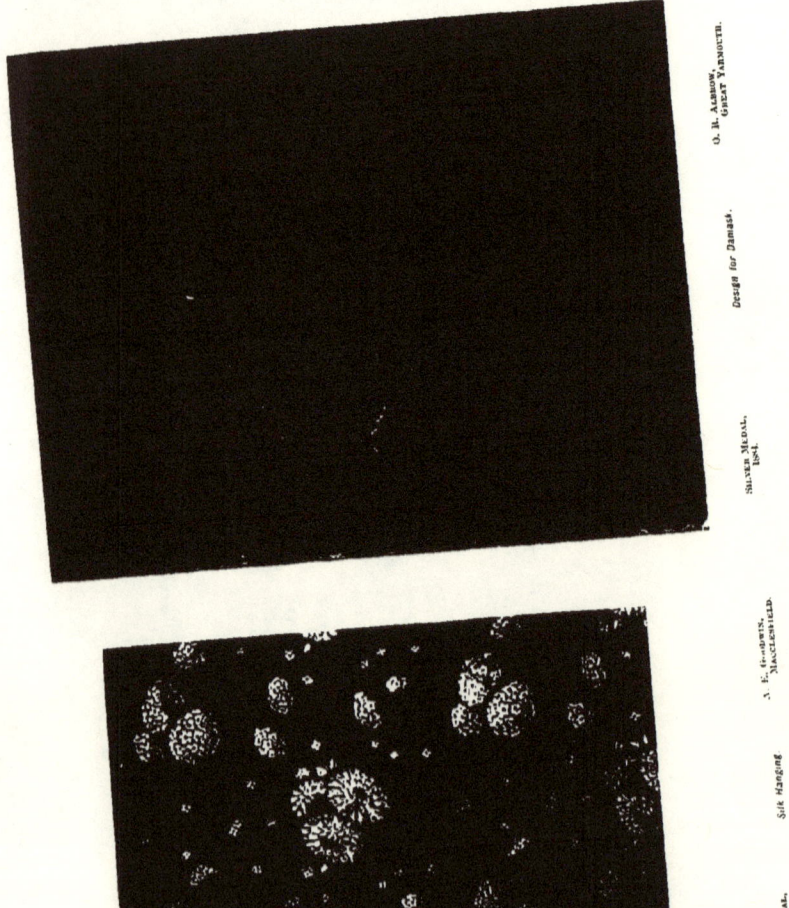

Design for Damask. O. H. ALDROW, GREAT YARMOUTH.
SILVER MEDAL, 1884.

Silk Hanging. A. E. GOODWIN, MACCLESFIELD.
SILVER MEDAL, 1884.

36

Sidney G. Mawson.
Manchester (Caversham St.)
Printed Cotton.
Gold Medal, Var. Nat.
1864.

C. Bassett, Macclesfield
Design for Silk Handkfs.
Silver Medal.
1864.

DESIGNS FOR CARPETS.

PLATES 37 TO 51.

GOLD MEDAL,
1888.
Carpet.
J. J. F. KING,
GLASGOW.

SILVER MEDAL, 1886.   Carpet.   A. W. L. DIXON, NOTTINGHAM.

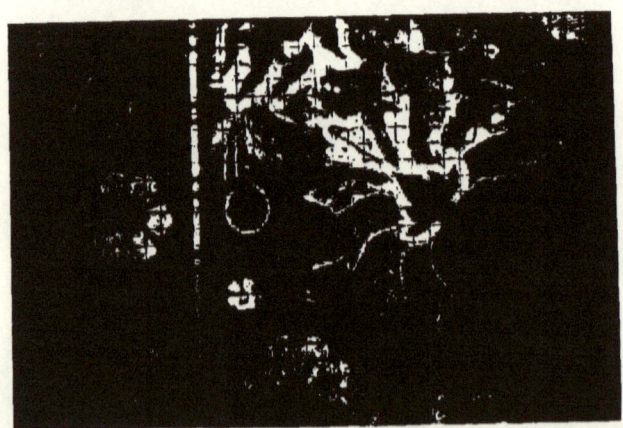

GOLD MEDAL, 1889.   Carpet.   J. J. F. KING, GLASGOW.

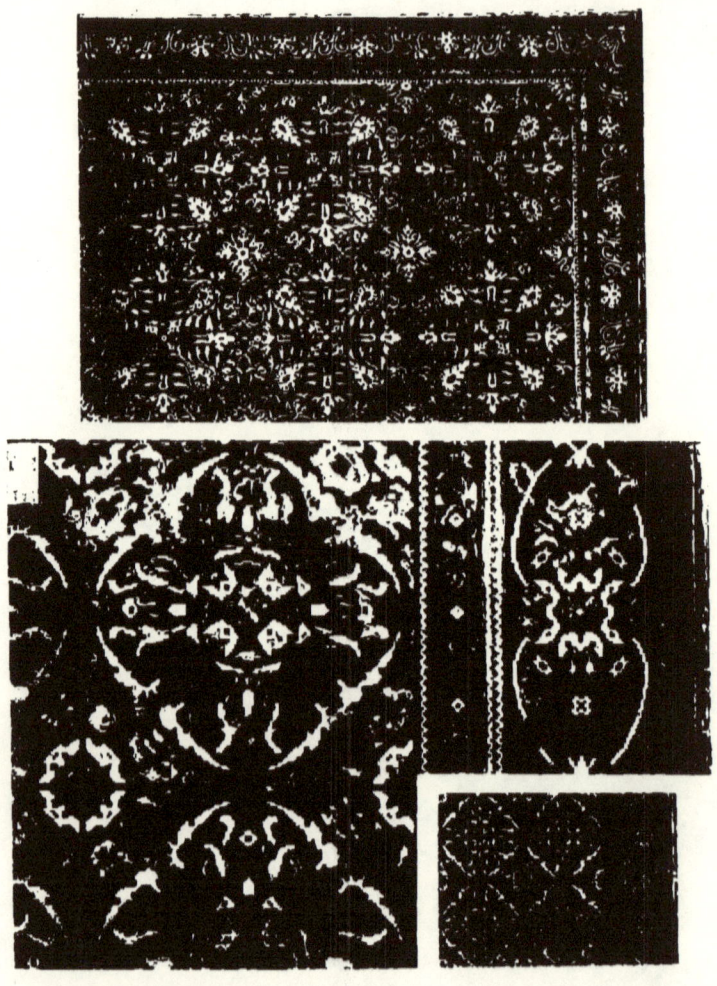

40

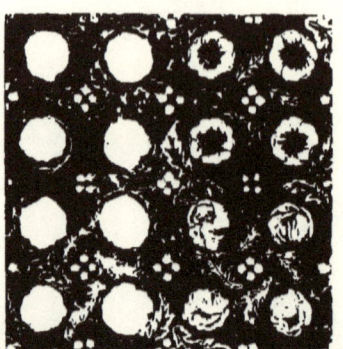

JAMES B. GLANVILLE, MANCHESTER.

Hanging.

SILVER MEDAL, 1867.

C. B. AYLWARD, SOUTH KENSINGTON.

Carpet.

GOLD MEDAL, 1864.

Carpet.

H. Allen,
Washington.

Gold Medal,
1876.

Silver Medal. Carpet. Arch. Walker.
1891. Glasgow.

Gold Medal (1vo), 1890.   Carpet Design.   A. Walker, Glasgow.

Silver Medal (1vo),   Carpet Design.   A. Walker, Glasgow.

44

J. R. Collinwood,
Batizska.

Carpets.

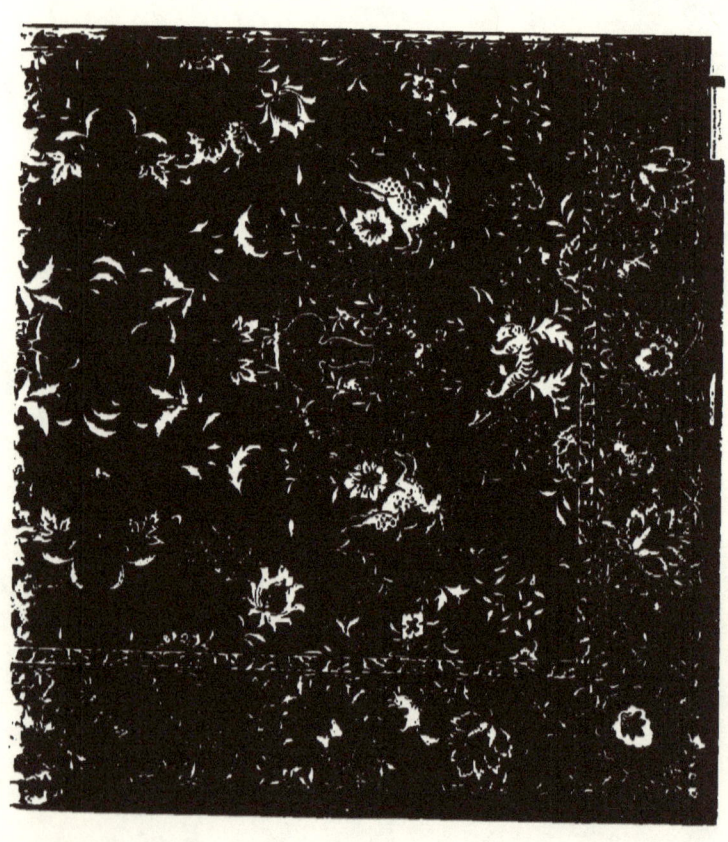

Gold Medal, 1890.   Carpet.   A. Walker, Glasgow.

47

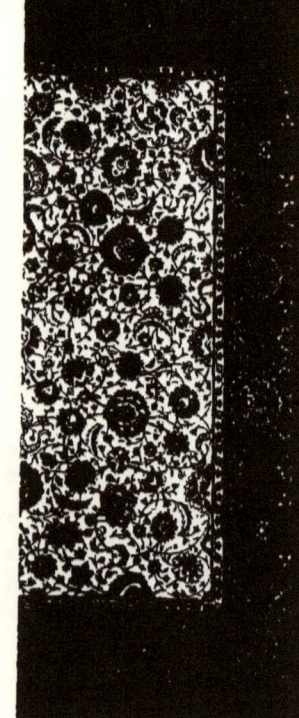

SILVER MEDAL,
1880.

J. FLETCHER,
GLASGOW.

48

Gold Medal. 1886.   Stair Carpet.   Margaret F. Jones, Manchester.

49

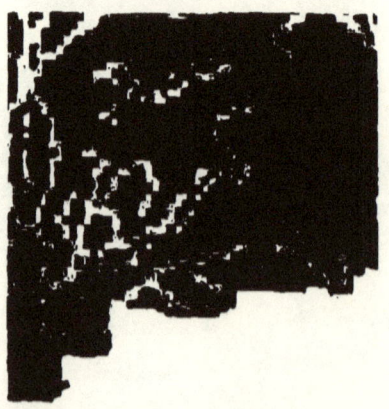

Gold Medal, 1880.   Carpet.   Herbert Cole, Manchester (Cavendish St.)

GOLD MEDAL, 1884.   *Design for Carpet.*   C. B. AYLWARD, SOUTH KENSINGTON.

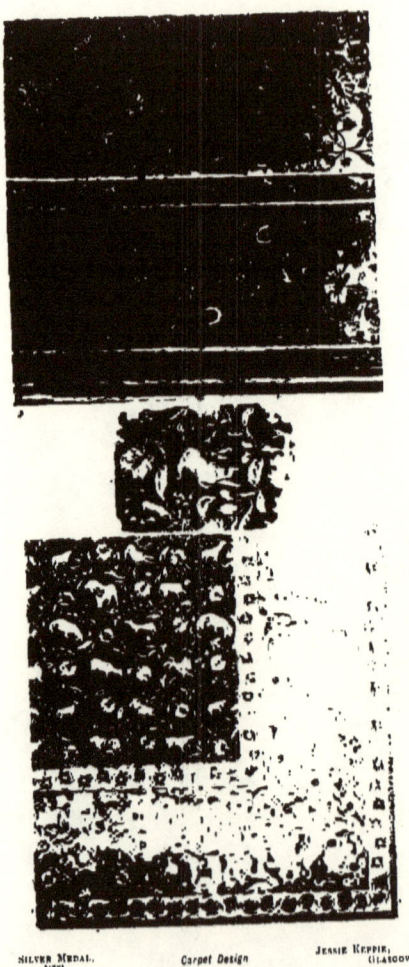

SILVER MEDAL, 1893.   Carpet Design   JESSIE KEPPIE, GLASGOW.

DESIGNS FOR WALL-PAPERS, Etc.

PLATES 52 TO 61.

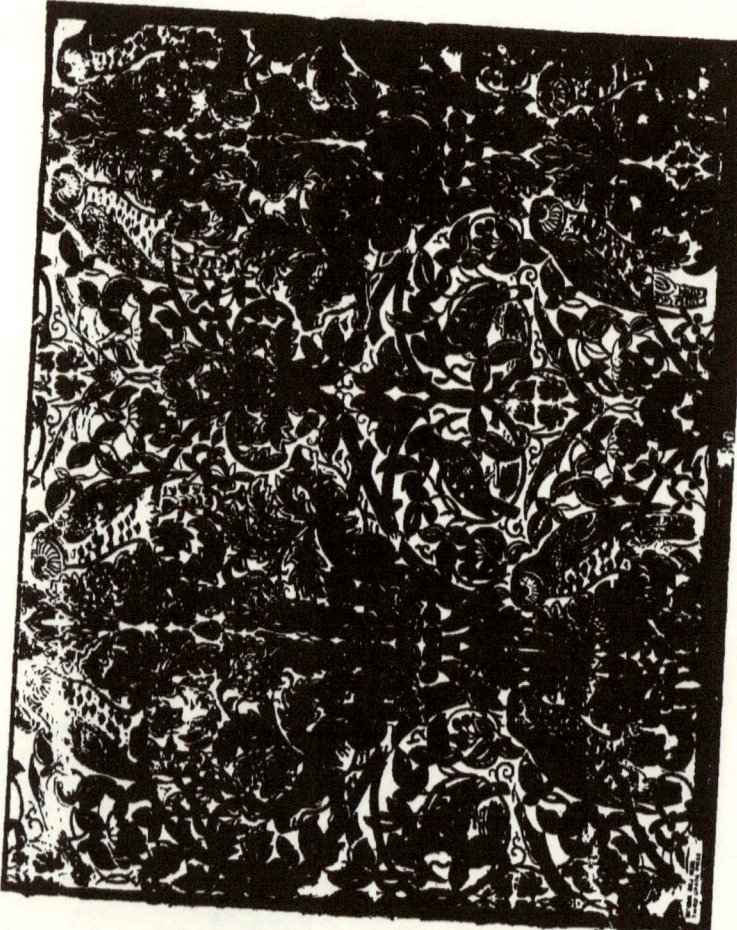

Design for Wall Paper.

S. G. Mawson,
Manchester.

J. Sampler,
Glasgow.
Silver Medal, 1893.

Designs for Wall Papers.

Designs for Wall Paper & Frieze.

Silver Medal, 1891.

A. A. Carpenter, London (Birkbeck Institute).

55

A. J. Corister,
London, (Birkbeck Institute).
Silver Medal, 1895.

Designs for Wall Papers.

W. Newstead,
Glasgow.
Silver Medal, 1892.

Maurice Strang, Glasgow. *Design for Wall Paper.* Gold Medal, 1902.

Design for Gate of Curtain.

T. A. Henny,
South Kensington.

Gold Medal,
1865.

Designs for Wall Papers

F. APPLEYARD,
SCARBORO'.

SILVER MEDAL,
1884.

Gold Medal, 1888.   *Design for Wall Paper.*   T. J. Donohue, Macclesfield.

SILVER MEDAL, 1904. Designs for Wall Paper and Frieze. CAROLINE THORNHILL, BLACKHEATH.

61

Oscar P. Mosler, Battersea. *Design for a Frieze.* Silver Medal, 1895.

J. H. Collingwood, Gosnell, B.N. *Painting of Ornament in Monochrome.* Silver Medal, 1893.

DESIGNS FOR
STAINED GLASS, FIGURE COMPOSITION, METAL WORK,
Etc.

Plates 62 to 72.

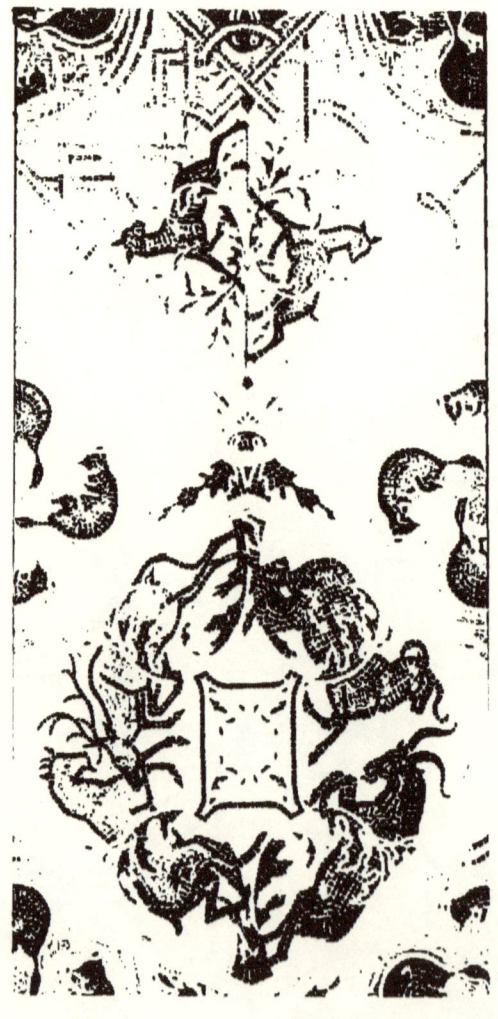

GERTRUDE BOOTH, CANTERBURY.
Design for a Mosaic Pavement.
GOLD MEDAL, 1891.

63

Mary K. Curtis, Canterbury.
Silver Medal, 1891.

Designs for Mosaic Pavements.

Mary K. Curtis, Canterbury.
Silver Medal, 1893.

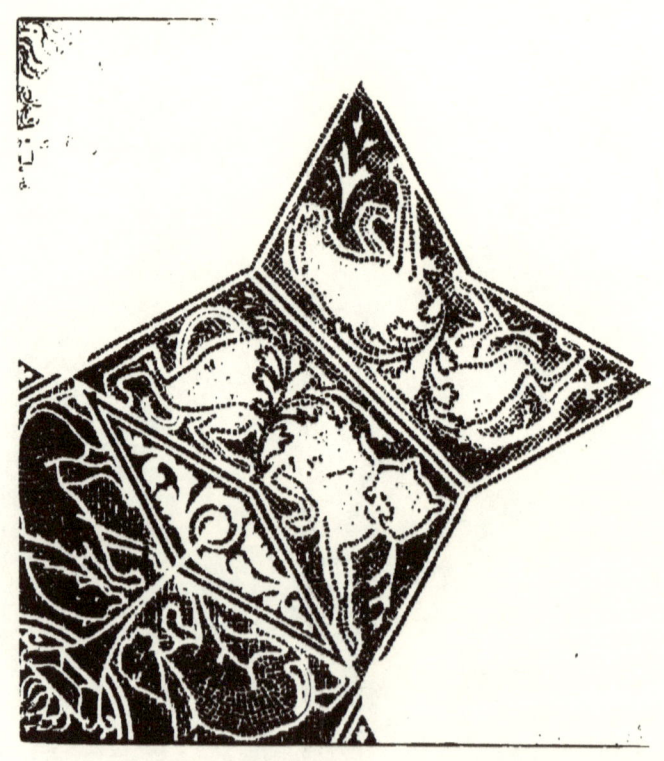

Gentile da Kirsti, Castlebury.

Design for a Mosaic Pavement

Gold Medal, 1902

Design for a Mosaic Pavement

Gold Medal, 1893

Mary Caldwell, Castlebury.

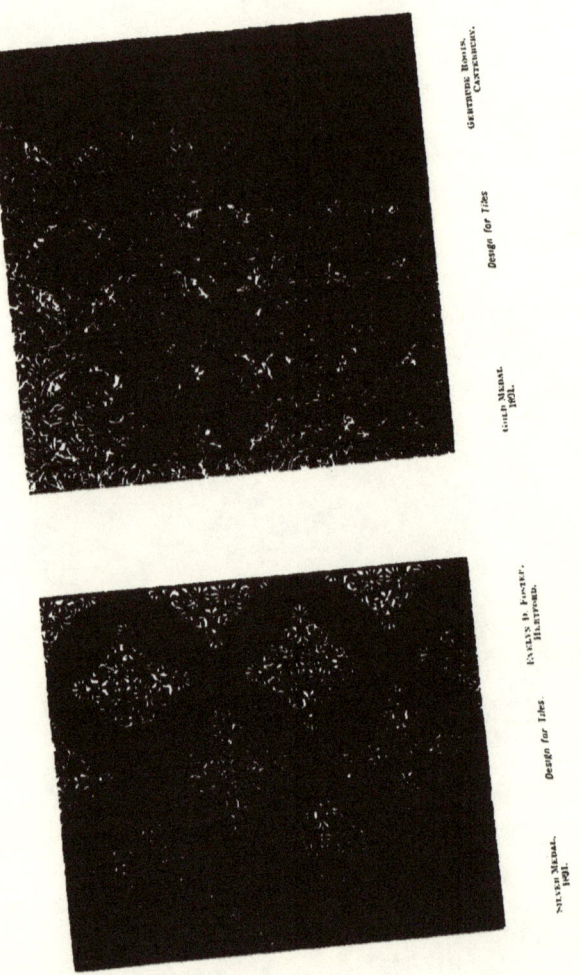

Design for Tiles. GERTRUDE BOOTH, CANTERBURY. GOLD MEDAL, 1891.

Design for Tiles. EVELYN B. FOSTER, HARTFORD. SILVER MEDAL, 1891.

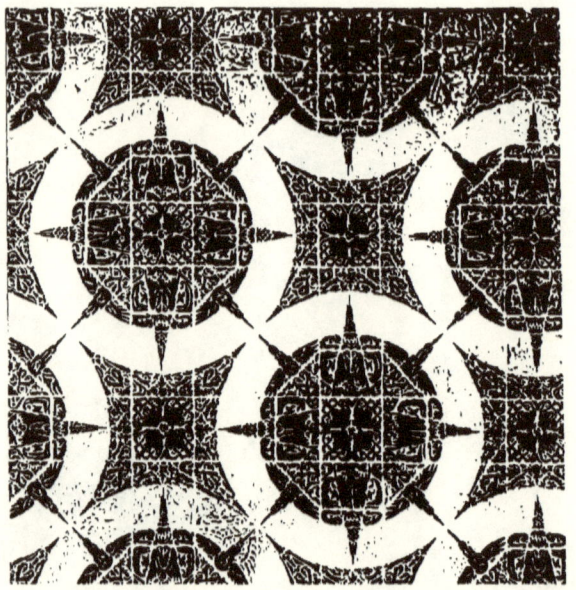

Design for Tiles. EMILY HAYTER. HERTFORD. SILVER MEDAL. 1887.

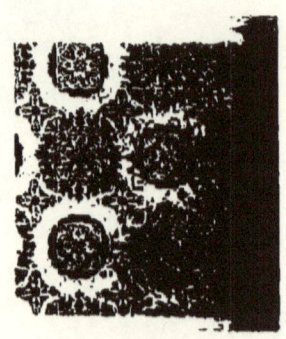

Design for Tiles. KYRIAN D. FOSTER. HERTFORD. SILVER MEDAL. 1886.

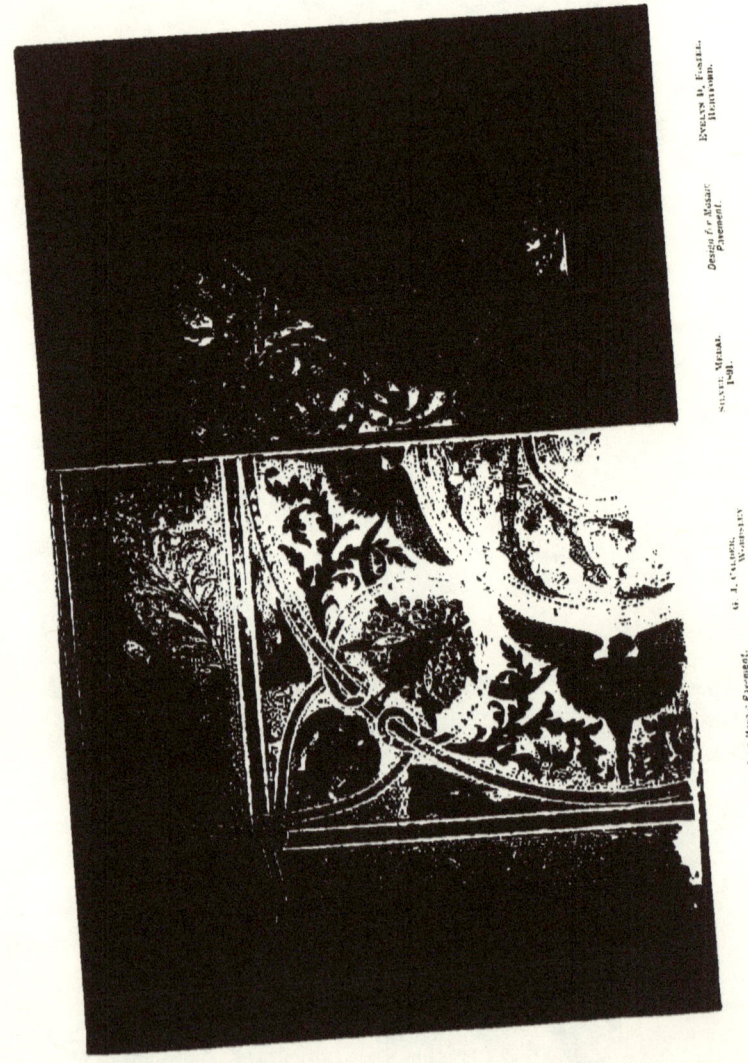

SIBYL MEIER, 1891. *Design for a Mosaic Pavement.*

G. J. GULDER, WORTLEY.

SIBYL MEIER, 1891. *Design for Mosaic Pavement.*

EVELYN B. FOSTER, HURSTMON.

72

Mary Morris, Canterbury.

Design for Tiles.

Silver Medal 1890.

DESIGNS FOR MOSAICS AND TILES.

Plates 73 to 86.

SILVER MEDAL, 1895. *Design for Stained Glass Window.* A. WALKER, GLASGOW. SILVER MEDAL, 1895. *Design for Window (small sketch).* AGNES MANLEY, BIRMINGHAM.

SILVER MEDAL, 1895.   MARY I. NEWILL, BIRMINGHAM.

SILVER MEDAL, 1895.   A. WALKER, GLASGOW.

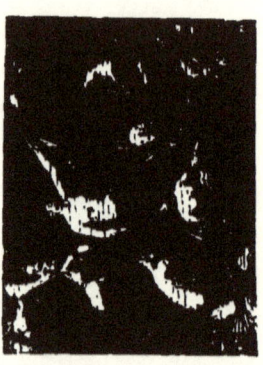

Silver Medal, 1893. Design with Figures. Kate Light, South Kensington.

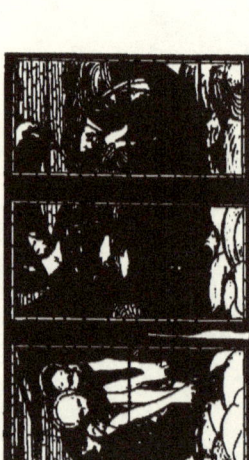
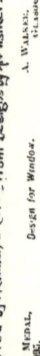

Silver Medal, 1896. Design for Window. A. Walker, Glasgow.

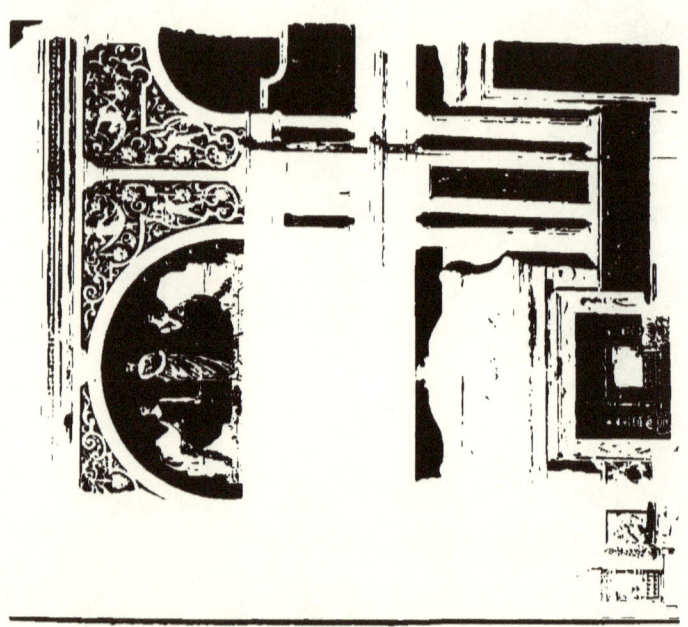

SILVER MEDAL．　　　　　Designs with Figures．　　　　　H. A. PAYNE.
1899.　　　　　　　　　　　　　　　　　　　　　　　　　BIRMINGHAM.

79

SILVER MEDAL,　　　　　Design for a Plateau.　　　FREDERICK SHELLEY,
1885.　　　　　　　　　　　　　　　　　　　　　　SOUTH KENSINGTON.

Alexandra Fisher,
South Kensington.

Plates showing adaptation of Statue by
M. Angelo.

Silver Medal,
1896.

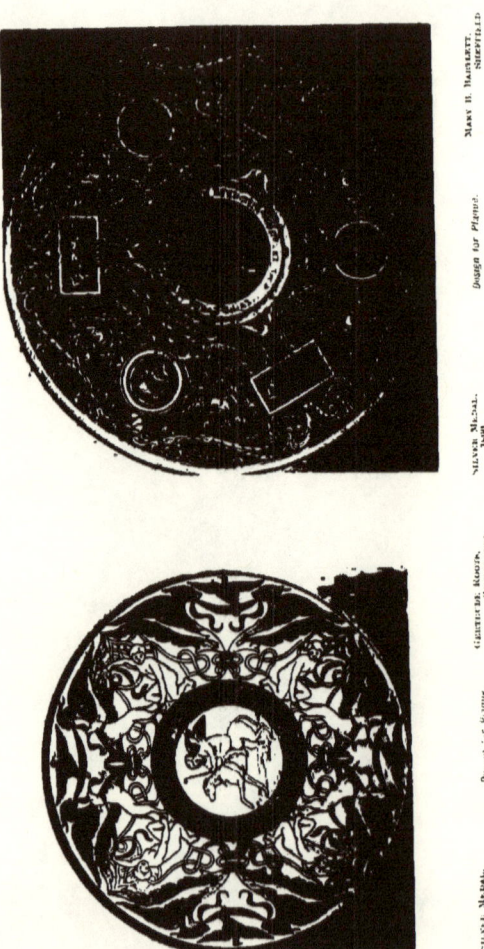

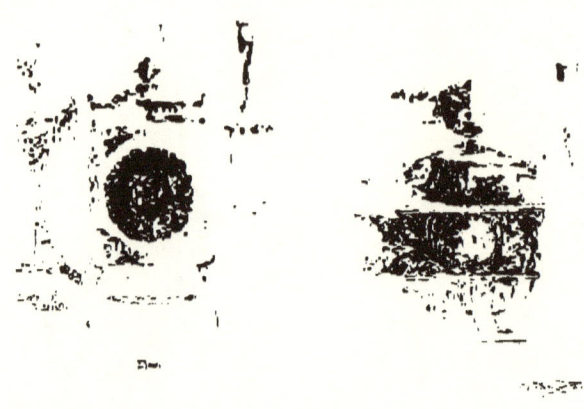

Designs for Silver Biscuit Box.

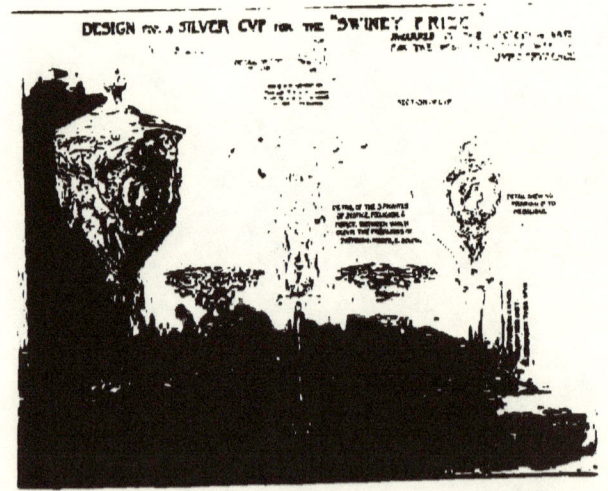

Silver Medal, 1893.

Design for Silver Cup.

W. A. Fenn,
New Cross.

SILVER MEDAL, 1896.   *Designs for Wrought Iron Garden Gates.*   J. MACFARLANE, MANCHESTER (Cavendish St.)

SILVER MEDAL, 1895.   *Design for Wrought Iron Gates.*   F. G. MOORE, MANCHESTER (Cavendish St.)

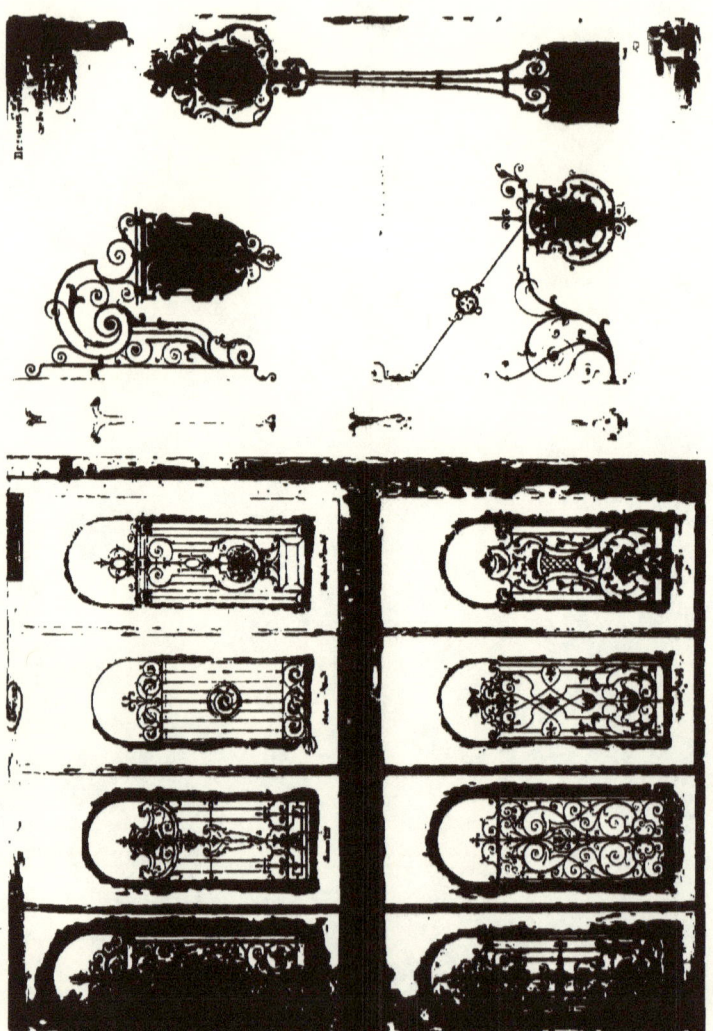

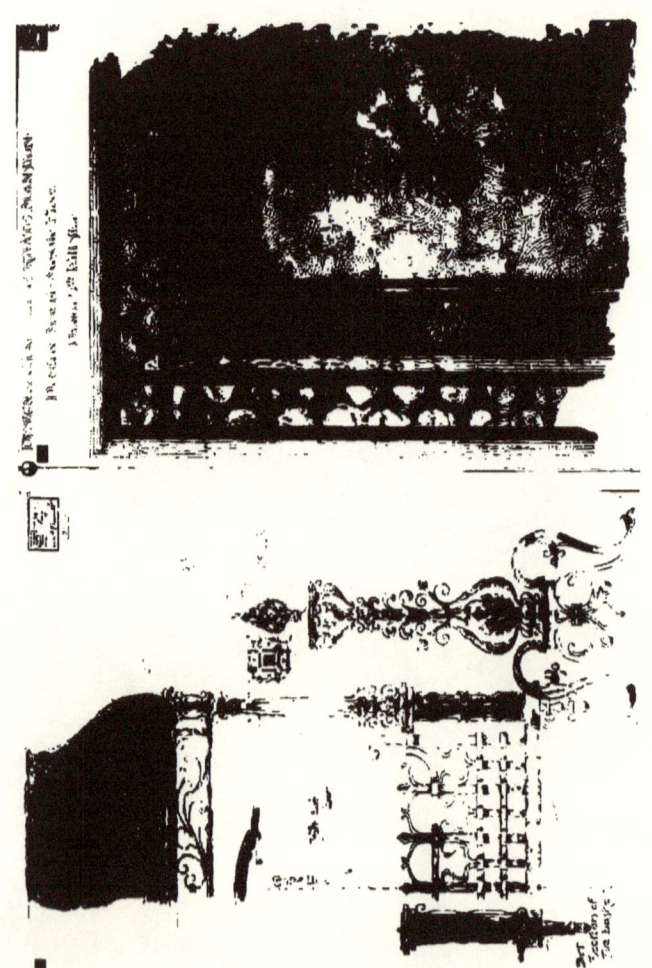

Details of Design of a Hall for a Private Mansion.

W. A. Fenn, New Cross.

Silver Medal, 1883.

SILVER MEDAL,
1891.

AMY HOBSON,
SHEFFIELD.

SILVER MEDAL,
1891.

Design for Jewel Casket and Candelabrum,
to be executed in Silver. Subject: Milton's l'Allegro.

F. STEELEY,
BIRMINGHAM.

PAINTINGS AND HISTORIC ORNAMENT.

Plates 87 to 105.

HONORARY AWARD.

SILVER MEDAL,
1880.
Portrait in Oil Colours
F. SUDDARDS,
SOUTH KESSINGTON.

Study of an Interior in Oil Colours

Gertrude Lane, Manchester

Gold Medal, 1891

SILVER MEDAL, 1891.   *Study in Watercolours.*   ROSIE C. WHITESIDE, BLOOMSBURY.

SILVER MEDAL, 1894.   *Ornament Painted in Monochrome*   F. W. CLOUGH, BRADFORD (*Church Institute*).

J. M. TWISS, SOUTH KENSINGTON.   *Ornament Painted in Monochrome*   SILVER MEDAL, 1894.

Studies for Decorative Purposes from Natural History Museum.

WILLIAM GOZA,
SOUTH KENSINGTON.

SILVER MEDAL,
1893.

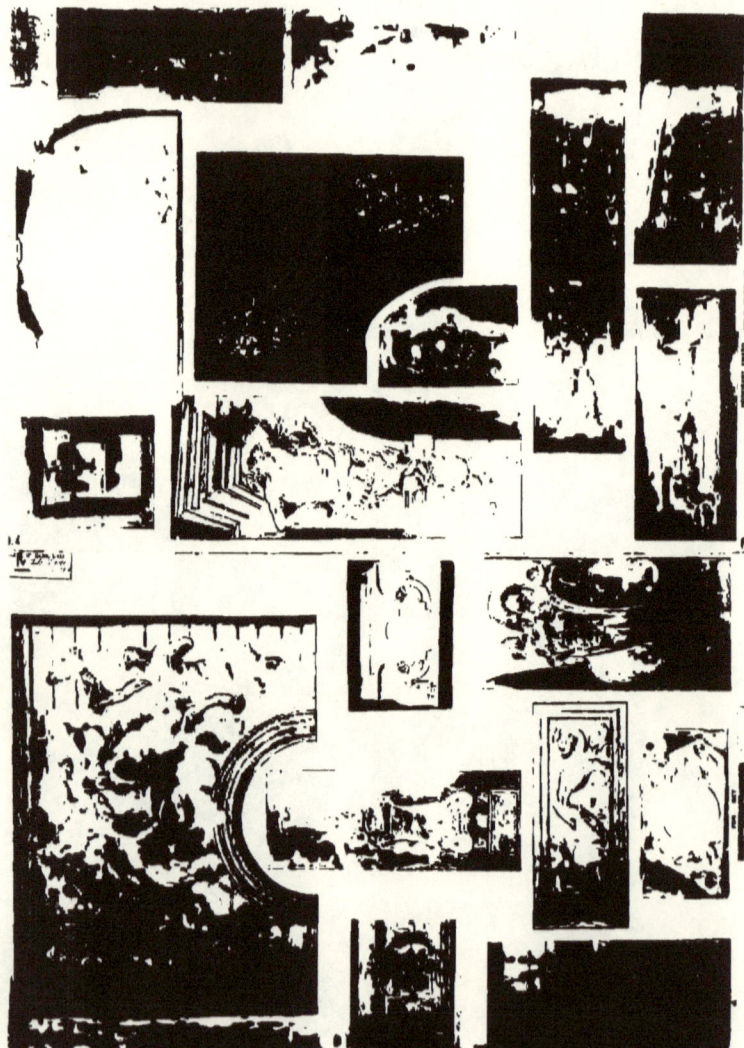

Studies of *Relief Ornaments.*

Silver Medal, 1881.

G. Cartlidge,
South Kensington.

SILVER MEDAL,
1891.

Studies of Decorative Figures.

G. CARTLIDGE,
SOUTH KENSINGTON.

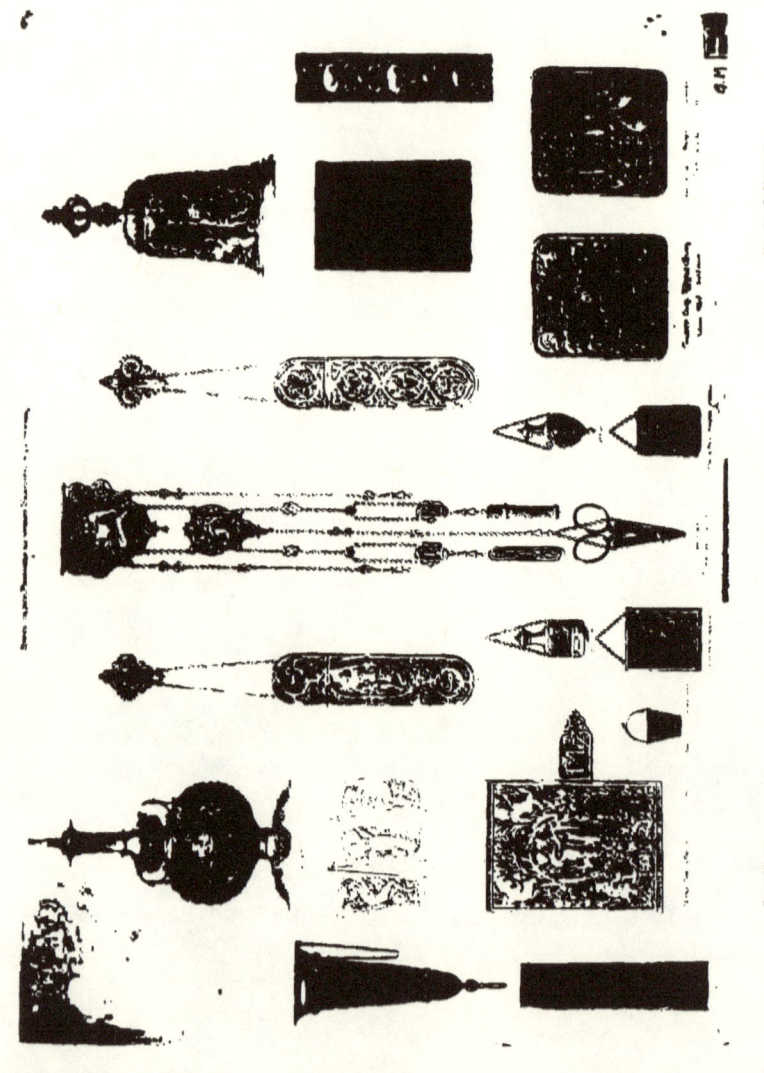

Gold Medal, 1895.   Studies of Gold and Silver Objects.   J. R. Duffield, Sheffield.

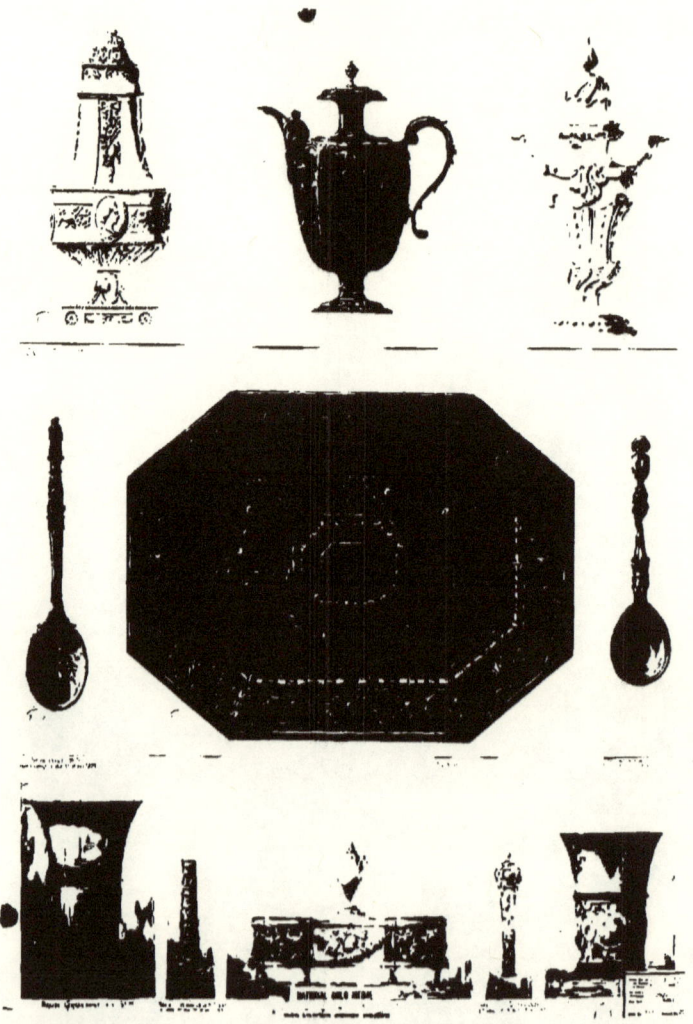

Gold Medal, 1895. Studies of Gold and Silver Objects. J. R. Duffield, Sheffield.

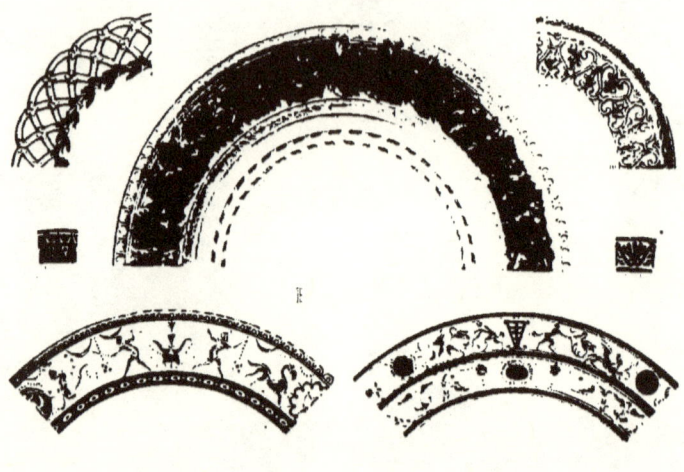

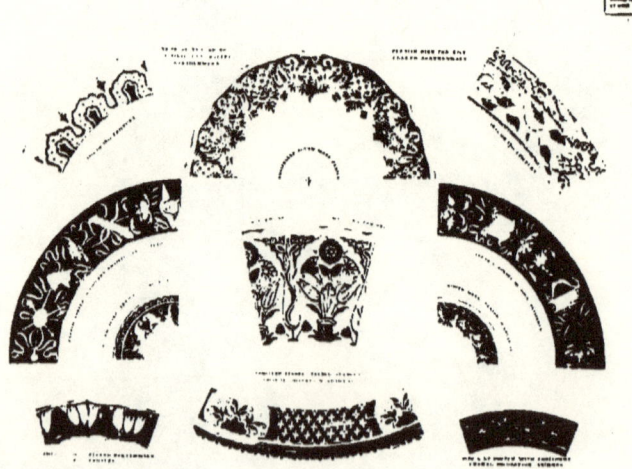

SILVER MEDAL, 1885. Studies of Pottery Borders. TRACY TRATMAN, SOUTH KENSINGTON.

100

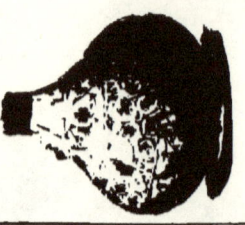

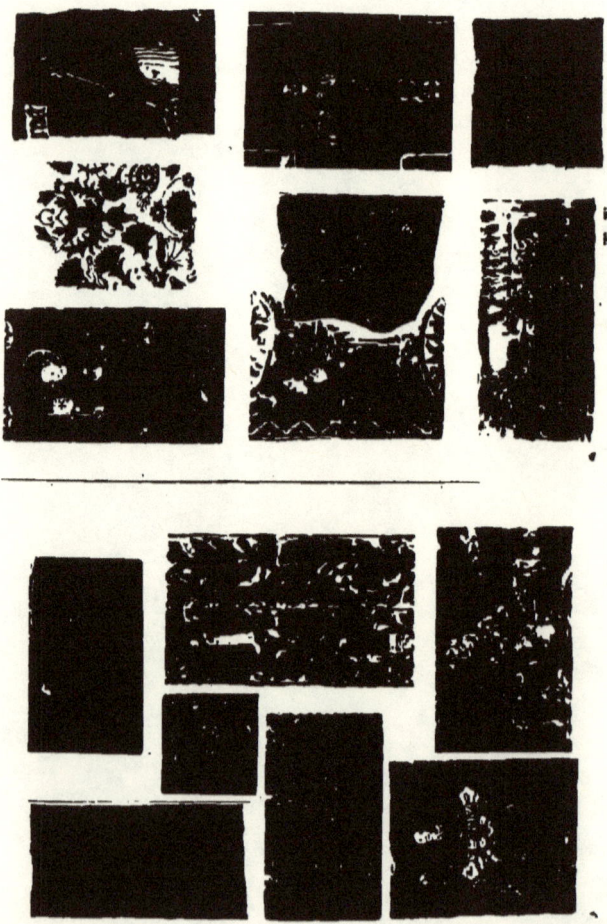

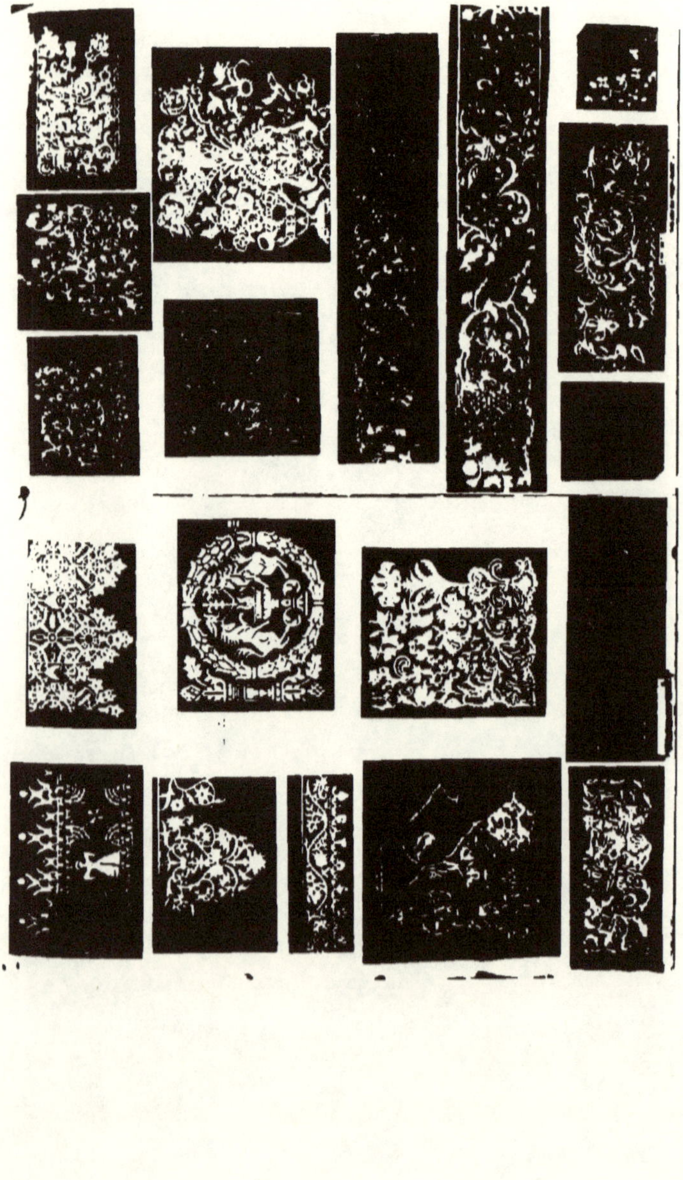

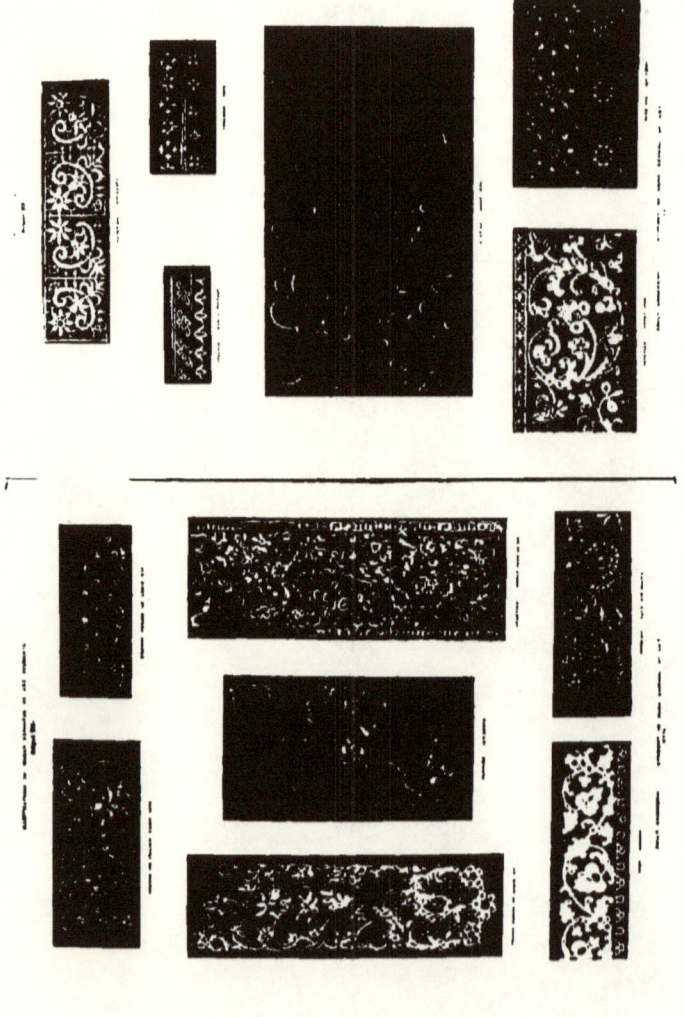

105

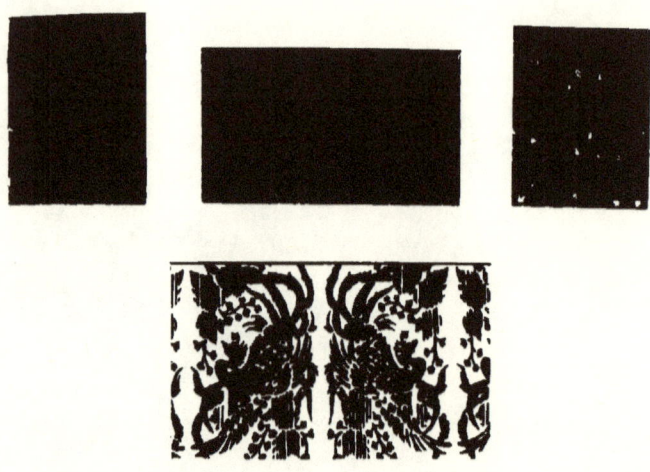

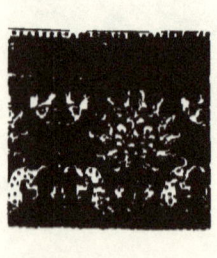  

SILVER MEDAL.   Historic Studies of Tapestry

LIFE DRAWINGS AND DRAPERY STUDIES.

Plates 106 to 123.

GOLD MEDAL.
1892.

Chalk Drawing from Life.

Gold Medal, 1894. Chalk Drawing from Life. Albert C. O. John, Hanley.

110

Gold Medal.
1893.
Chalk Drawing from Life.
Annie L. Henderson

SILVER MEDAL, 1884.   Chalk Drawing from Life.   KENNETH M. (...)
    LIVERPOOL

SILVER MEDAL, 1884.   Chalk Drawing from Life.

SILVER MEDAL, W. H. KNIGHT, Chalk Drawing from life
1905 BIRMINGHAM.

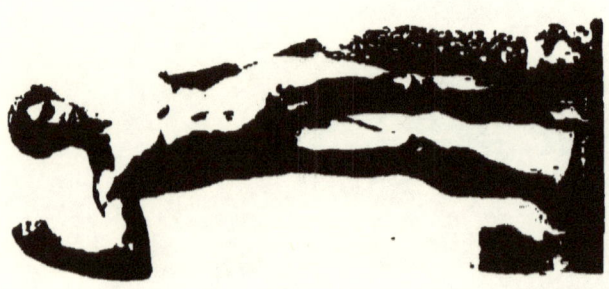

Studies of Drapery in Chalk

110

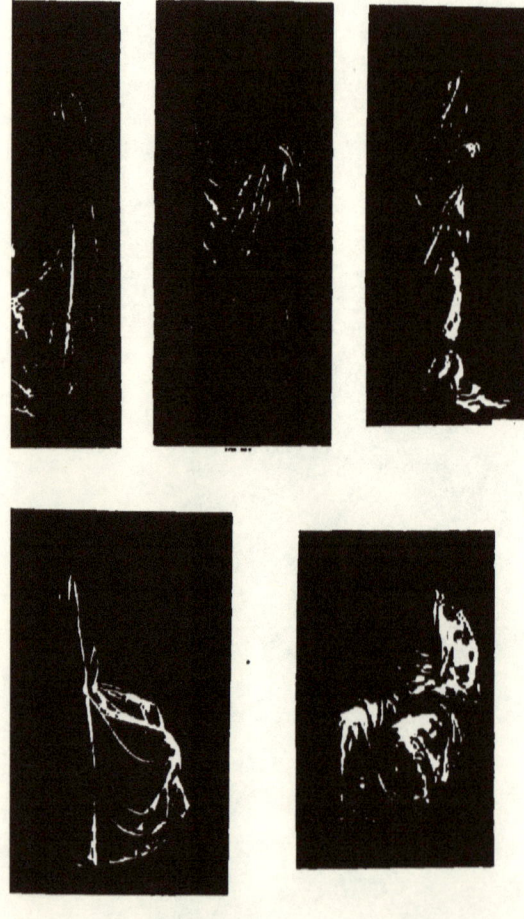

Chalk Studies of Drapery

121

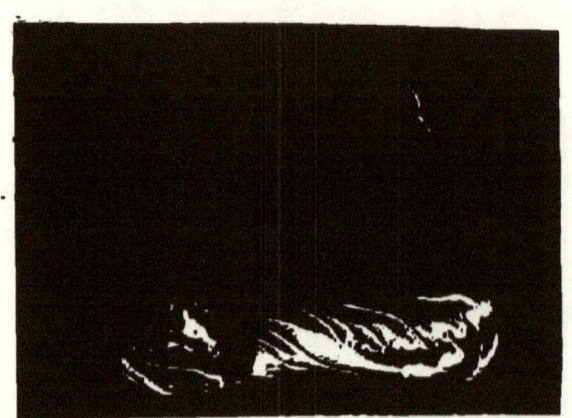

SILVER MEDAL,
1891.   Chalk Studies of Drapery   FRANCIS A. B. ...
                                        VANCOUVER

SILVER MEDAL,
1899.   Chalk Studies of Drapery   H. K. ...

GOLD MEDAL
1885.
Chalk Study of Drapery.
W. L. PALTRIDGE,
BIRMINGHAM.

SILVER MEDAL, 1895. *Chalk Study of Drapery.* LOUISA BUTCHER WAKEFIELD.

SILVER MEDAL. *Chalk Study of Drapery.* MOLLY WOOD, LEA RD.

MODELLED DESIGNS AND FIGURE STUDIES.

Plates 124 to 156.

Gold Medal, 1891. — Modelled Design for a Gold and Silver Goblet. — Eleanor L. Mercer, Sheffield.

GOLD MEDAL, 1895.   *Modelled Design for a Bronze Candlestick.*   M. LILIAN SIMPSON, SOUTH KENSINGTON.

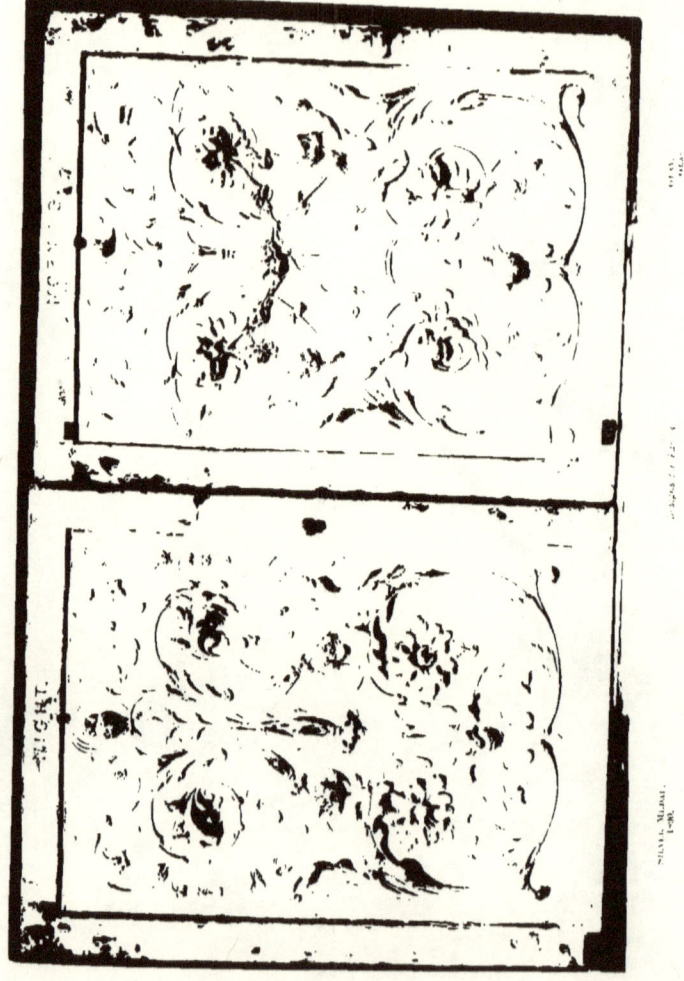

Silver Medal, 1890.   Modelled Study   F. Carder, Wordsley.   Silver Medal, 1895.   Modelled Design for a Silver Goblet.   Florence Steele, South Kensington.

GOLD MEDAL.   *Modelled Design for a Panel*   PETER McCROSSAN, SOUTH KENSINGTON.

GOLD MEDAL, 1895. *Decorative Modelled Figure.* MARGARET GILES, SOUTH KENSINGTON.

130

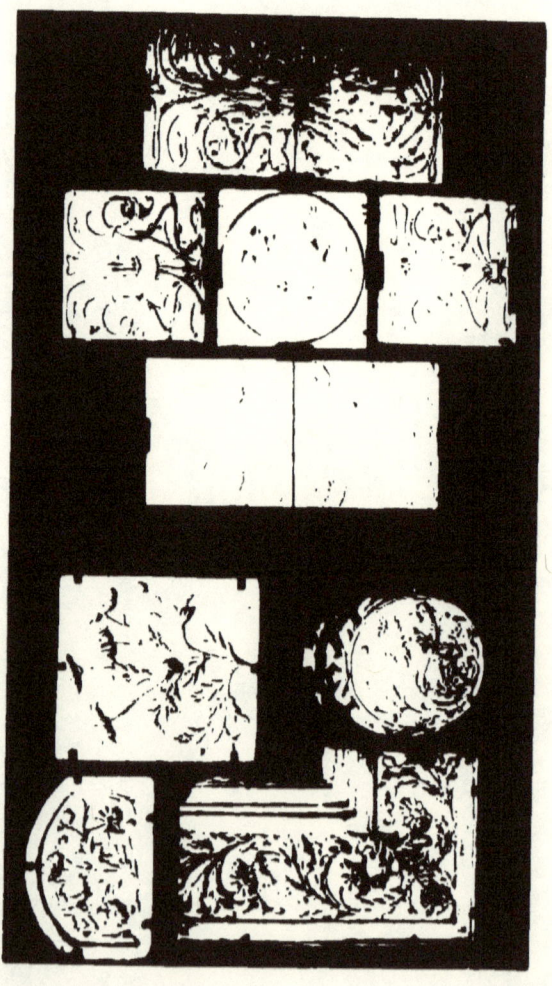

A. Mills,
South Kensington.
Silver Medal, 1905.

Monochrome Studies, Draped from Life.

Jane M. Thur,
South Kensington.
Silver Medal, 1905.

136

SILVER MEDAL, 1904. — Modelled Wall Tiles. — S. ANNIE WILLIS, PLYMOUTH (Technical School).

SILVER MEDAL, 1902. — Modelled Panel. — GEORGIE C. FRANCE, BIRMINGHAM.

138

130

140

ESTHER MOORE,
SOUTH KENSINGTON,
SILVER MEDAL, 1893.

Decorative Modelled Figures

LILIAN SIMPSON,
SOUTH KENSINGTON,
SILVER MEDAL, 1893.

142

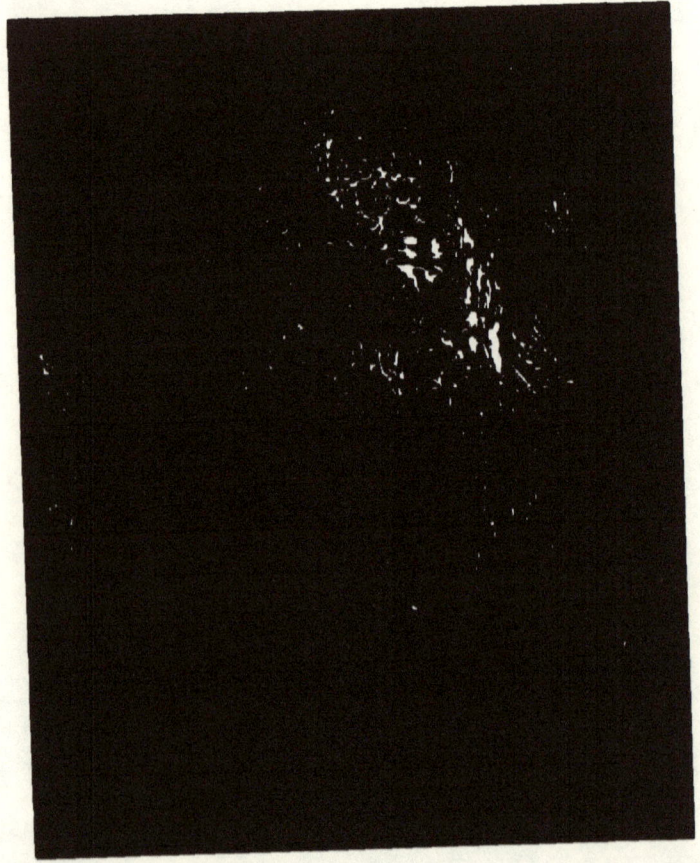

Lantern. Willoughby, Plymouth (Technical School)

Modelled Wax Decoration

Gold Medal, 1895.

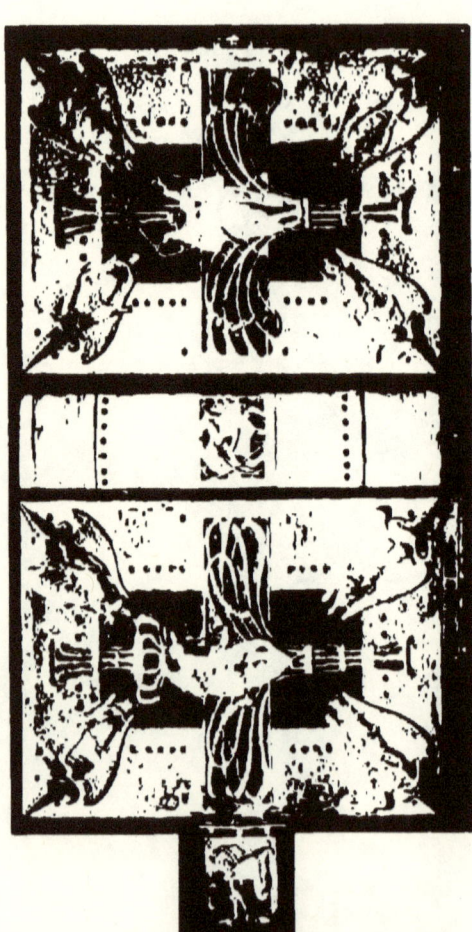

144

146

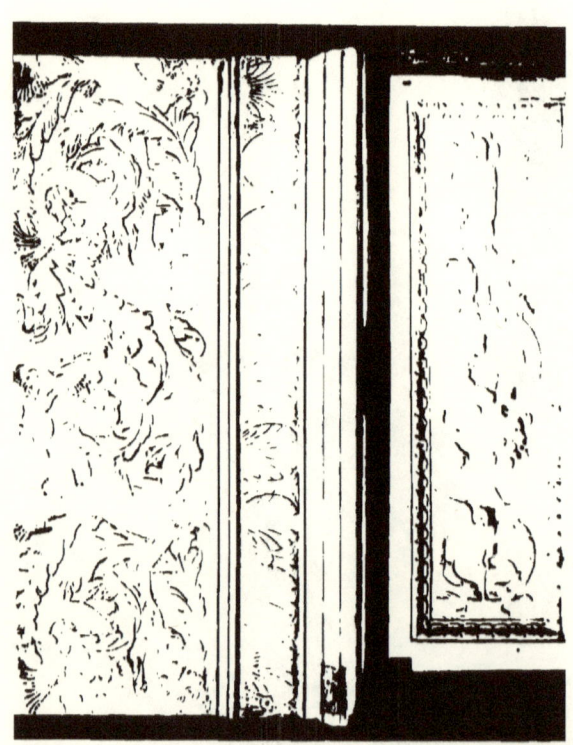

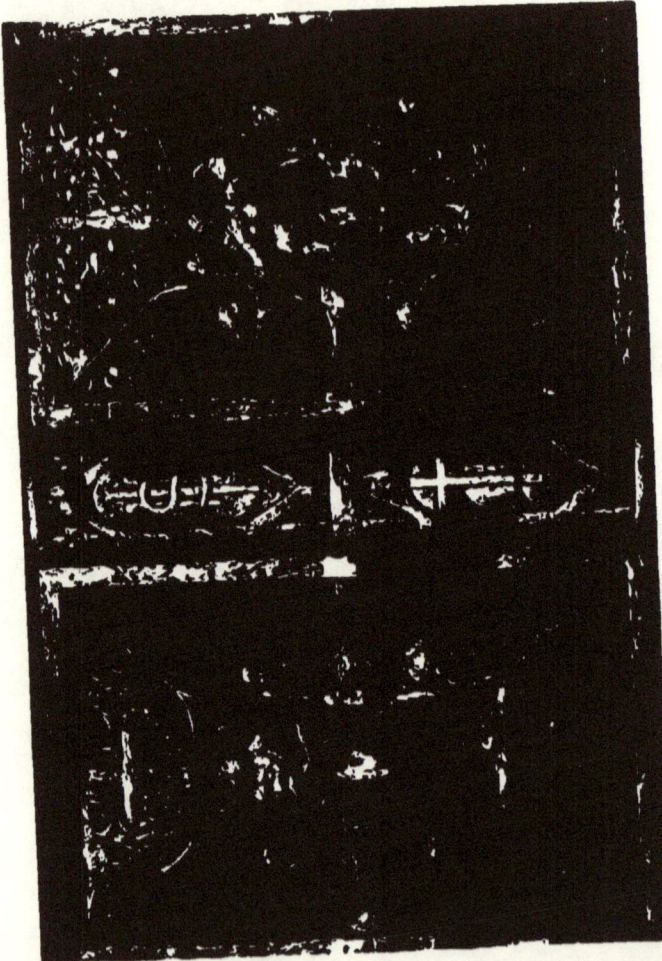

149

SILVER MEDAL. Vase of Flowers. C. W. McKechnie
1889.

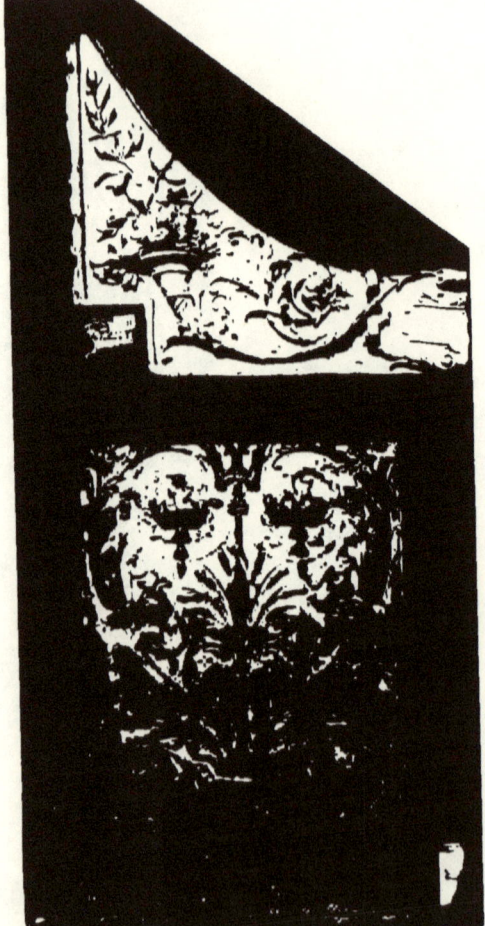

SILVER MEDAL. Spray Panel. FREDERICK BUTLER,
1884. LAMBETH.

151

SILVER MEDAL, 1896. Portion of Pediment for over a Door. ANNA DAVIS, SOUTH KENSINGTON.

SILVER MEDAL, 1896. Panel representing Commerce J. CASSIDY, MANCHESTER.

Gold Medal, 1890.   Decorative Modelled Panel.   David McNair, South Kensington.

154

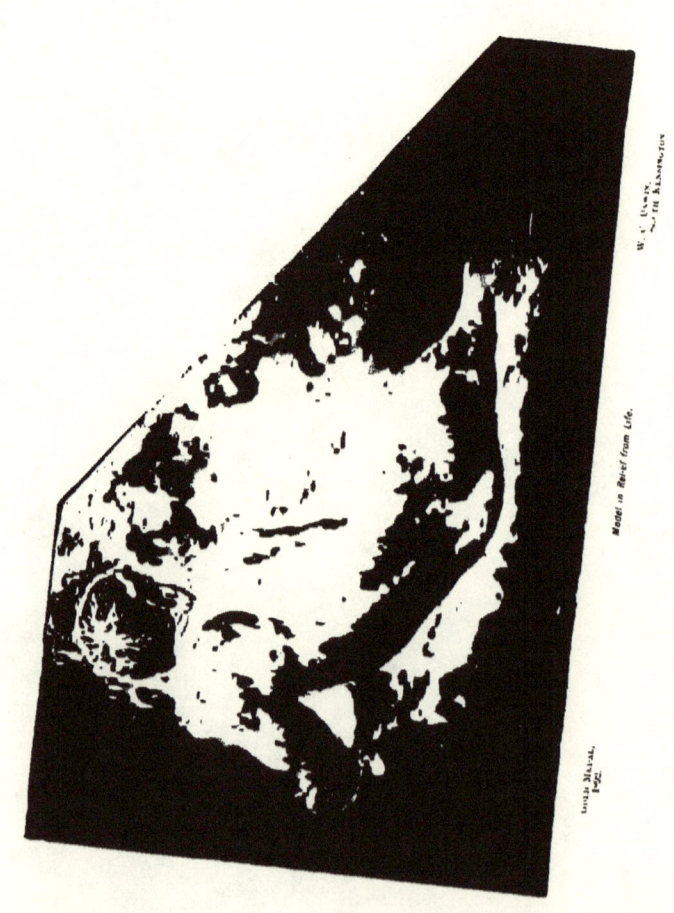

Model in Relief from Life.

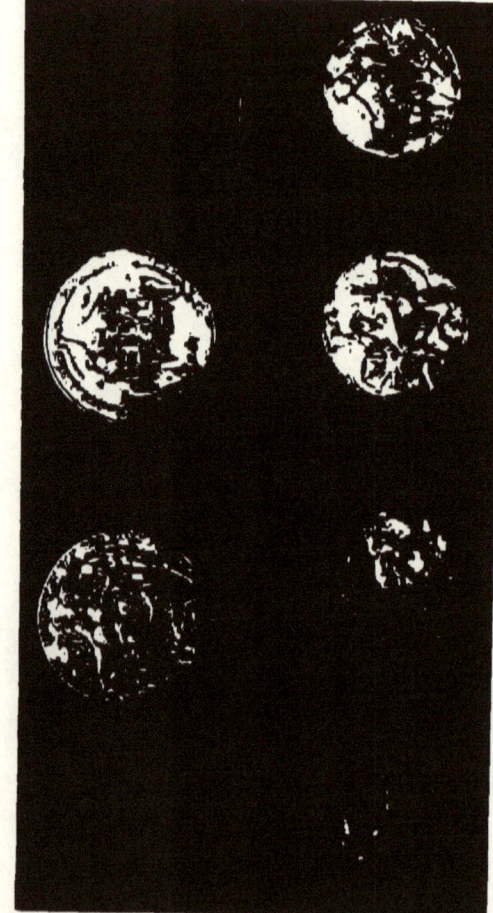

www.ingramcontent.com/pod-product-compliance
Lightning Source LLC
Chambersburg PA
CBHW030004240426
43672CB00007B/824